Summer Quest!™

Summer Workbook Series

Note: All activities with young children should be performed with adult supervision. Caregivers should be aware of allergies, sensitivities, health, and safety issues.

Credit

Production: Shakespeare Squared LLC

Rainbow Bridge
An imprint of Carson-Dellosa Publishing LLC
P.O. Box 35665
Greensboro, NC 27425 USA

ISBN 978-1-60095-386-6

Table of Contents

Encouraging Summer Reading

Literacy is the single most important skill that your child needs to be successful in school. The following list includes ideas of ways that you can help your child discover the great adventures of reading!

- Establish a time for reading each day. Ask your child about what he or she is reading. Try to relate the material to an event that is happening this summer or to another book or story.

- Let your child see you reading for enjoyment. Talk about the great things that you discover when you read.

- Create a summer reading list. Choose books from the reading list (pages v–vi) or head to the library and explore the shelves. A general rule for selecting books at the appropriate reading level is to choose a page and ask your child to read it aloud. If he or she does not know more than five words on the page, the book may be too difficult.

- Read newspaper and magazine articles, recipes, menus, maps, and street signs on a daily basis to show your child the importance of reading.

- Find books that relate to your child's experiences. For example, if you are going camping, find a book about camping. This will help your child develop new interests.

- Visit the library each week. Let your child choose his or her own books, but do not hesitate to ask your librarian for suggestions. Often, librarians can recommend books based on what your child enjoyed in the past.

- Make up stories. This is especially fun to do in the car, on camping trips, or while waiting at the airport. Encourage your child to tell a story with a beginning, a middle, and an end. Or, have your child start a story and let other family members build on it.

- Encourage your child to join a summer reading club at the library or a local bookstore. Your child may enjoy talking to other children about the books that he or she has read.

Summer Reading List

The summer reading list includes fiction and nonfiction titles. Experts recommend that second- and third-grade students read for at least 20 minutes each day. Then, ask questions about the story to reinforce comprehension.

Anno, Masaichiro and Mitsumasa
Anno's Mysterious Multiplying Jar

Blume, Judy
The Pain and the Great One

Bunting, Eve
So Far from the Sea

Burns, Marilyn
Spaghetti and Meatballs for All!

Carle, Eric
The Tiny Seed

Chbosky, Stacy
Who Owns the Sun?

Cherry, Lynne
The Great Kapok Tree: A Tale of the Amazon Rain Forest

Christian, Peggy
If You Find a Rock

Cleary, Beverly
Romana the Pest

Curtis, Gavin
The Bat Boy and His Violin

DeGross, Monalisa
Donovan's Word Jar

dePaola, Tomie
The Art Lesson

Dobson, David
Can We Save Them? Endangered Species of North America

DK Publishing
Eye Wonder: Mammals
Eye Wonder: Invention

Estes, Eleanor
The Hundred Dresses

Falwell, Cathryn
Word Wizard

George, Jean Craighead
The Tarantula in My Purse and 172 Other Wild Pets

Gibbons, Gail
Nature's Green Umbrella

Goldish, Meish
Does the Moon Change Shape

Hopkinson, Deborah
Sweet Clara and the Freedom Quilt

Keats, Ezra Jack
Peter's Chair

Summer Reading List (continued)

Lester, Helen
Author: A True Story

Locker, Thomas
Water Dance

MacLachlan, Patricia
All the Places to Love

Palatini, Margie
Bedhead
Sweet Tooth

Parish, Peggy
Amelia Bedelia

Pilkey, Dav
Dog Breath

Polacco, Patricia
Thunder Cake

Rylant, Cynthia
An Angel for Solomon Singer

Say, Allen
Grandfather's Journey

Schotter, Roni
*Nothing Ever Happens on
    90th Street*

Schwartz, David M.
How Much Is a Million?

Scieszka, Jon
Math Curse
*The True Story of the Three
    Little Pigs*

Seuss, Dr.
The Lorax

Shasha, Mark
Night of the Moonjellies

Silverstein, Shel
A Light in the Attic

Steig, William
Brave Irene

Storad, Conrad J.
*Lizards for Lunch:
    A Roadrunner's Tale*

Titus, Eve
Basil of Baker Street

Uchida, Yoshiko
The Bracelet

Van Allsburg, Chris
The Polar Express

Waber, Bernard
Lyle, Lyle, Crocodile

Walker, Sarah
Eye Wonder: Dinosaur

Williams, Margery
The Velveteen Rabbit

Wisniewski, David
*The Secret Knowledge of
    Grown-Ups*

Skills Checklist

With this book, your child will have the opportunity to practice and acquire many new skills. Keep track of the skills you practice together. Put a check beside each skill your child completes.

Math

- [ ] addition
- [ ] calendar skills
- [ ] division
- [ ] fact families
- [ ] fractions
- [ ] geometry
- [ ] graphs and grids
- [ ] measurement
- [ ] money
- [ ] multiplication
- [ ] numbers
- [ ] patterns
- [ ] place value
- [ ] probability
- [ ] story problems
- [ ] subtraction
- [ ] symmetry
- [ ] telling time

Language Arts

- [ ] alphabetizing
- [ ] composition
- [ ] dictionary skills
- [ ] grammar
- [ ] handwriting
- [ ] parts of speech
- [ ] phonics
- [ ] punctuation
- [ ] reading comprehension
- [ ] sentence structure
- [ ] spelling
- [ ] vocabulary
- [ ] word parts

Skills Checklist (continued)

Physical Fitness/Health

☐ endurance   ☐ strength building

☐ hygiene   ☐ stretching

Social Studies

☐ character development   ☐ government

☐ communities   ☐ map skills

☐ geography

Science

☐ biology   ☐ geology

☐ experiment   ☐ temperature

▶ **Circle the correct numeral for each number word.**

1. forty-five

   54   45

2. fifty-eight

   58   85

3. eighty-one

   18   81

4. thirty

   30   31

5. three

   30   3

6. fifteen

   15   50

▶ **Write the number word for each numeral.**

7. 0: _____

8. 60: _____

9. 40: _____

10. 30: _____

11. 20: _____

12. 80: _____

13. 70: _____

14. 50: _____

Take a watch outside and find an anthill. Look at the ants go in and out of the anthill for ten minutes. Count how many ants you see going in and out. What do they do if you put a few cookie crumbs near their home?

► A **noun** is a person, place, or thing. Write each noun from the word bank in the correct column.

aunt	cloud	friend
letter	plate	shoe
city	desert	gym
officer	prince	store

Person	**Place**	**Thing**
_____	_____	_____
_____	_____	_____
_____	_____	_____
_____	_____	_____

Make a secret code! Write the letters of the alphabet down one side of a piece of paper. Next to each letter, write a different symbol, such as a circle, star, or heart. A computer keyboard is a good place to get ideas for symbols. Now use the symbols to write a coded message and give it to a friend. Can she decode your message?

▶ **Read each word aloud. Write the number of syllables you hear. Then, write the number of vowel sounds you hear.**

Word	Syllables	Vowel Sounds
Example: rabbit	2	2
1. three		
2. red		
3. window		
4. elephant		
5. playful		
6. lady		
7. favorite		
8. nine		
9. truck		

Go trail blazing. Cut a piece of colorful fabric into strips. As you take a walk, tie the strips to branches, signposts, or fences. Make sure you can see the last strip as you tie a new one. Take a friend on a walk, and follow the same route to see if your friend can follow the trail. Clean up the strips when you finish.

3

▶ **Circle the correct numeral for each number word.**

1. forty-four

    4   44

2. sixty-two

    62   26

3. twenty-one

    12   21

4. fifty

    50   55

5. three

    30   3

6. fifteen

    15   50

▶ **Write the number words for the following numerals:**

0	20	30	40	60	80

_____   _____

_____   _____

_____   _____

Stand a stick in a lump of clay and place it on a sunny sidewalk. Trace its shadow with chalk. Go back an hour later and trace the shadow again. What happened to the shadow?

4

► **Read each word in the word bank. Write the** *soft c* **words under the celery. Write the** *hard c* **words under the carrot.**

cake	cell
century	cave
coat	city
cat	cent

celery

carrot

_____ _____

_____ _____

_____ _____

With an adult, go outside and look at the stars. Ancient Greeks imagined lines between the stars that made pictures. Can you imagine a star picture? Draw the picture on a piece of paper in the dark. Did it turn out like you imagined?

▶ **A cardinal number tells** *how many* **or** *how much* **and can be written as a numeral (***80***) or as a number word (***eighty***). An ordinal number tells the position of an item in a series (***eightieth***). Fill in the chart with the cardinal numerals, cardinal number words, or ordinal number words.**

	Cardinal Numeral	Cardinal Number Word	Ordinal Number Word
1.	20		
2.		sixty	
3.		thirty-six	
4.	77		
5.			fifth

Go on a texture hunt. Peel the paper off of a dark crayon. Grab a piece of paper and head outside. Put the paper on tree trunks, sidewalks, and patio furniture. Rub the crayon over the paper. Ask a friend to guess where each rubbing came from.

▶ **Circle the nouns in each sentence. The number in parentheses tells how many nouns are in each sentence.**

1. The boy found a pink and white shell at the beach. (3)

2. My aunt owns a store in the country. (3)

3. The cloud is shaped like a rabbit. (2)

4. The letter is from my friend. (2)

5. The girl put the glass in the kitchen. (3)

6. The kite sailed with the breeze. (2)

7. Anna read a book about manatees. (3)

8. Owen and Cass hiked past the cave. (3)

Build a water village. Gather some plastic blocks and a big, shallow pan of water. Build towers and buildings in the water. Pour water over the tower and see where it falls.

7

▶ Draw lines to connect syllables to form complete words.

1.			
pen	met		
sun	cil		
hel	on		
drag	dae		

2.			
blos	som		
rab	der		
spi	bit		
ti	ger		

3.			
car	en		
pup	rot		
can	py		
sev	dy		

4.			
won	ry		
sum	der		
crick	mer		
mar	et		

5.			
can	cus		
pen	fin		
muf	dle		
cir	cil		

6.			
pea	dow		
dol	lar		
mit	ten		
win	nut		

Draw a picture of your bedroom as if you are looking at it from above. Draw windows, doors, and furniture. Next, draw your room again. Put the furniture in new places. Have an adult help change your room to match your drawing.

▶ Stand and Stretch

Test your flexibility with this stretching challenge. Remember to stretch slowly. It takes practice to improve flexibility.

Stand tall and hold a ruler in one hand. Bend slowly at the waist. Reach down until the tip of the ruler touches the ground. Check the ruler to find how close you are to touching the ground. If you can already touch the ground, try to flatten your hands to the floor. Stretch three times. Record your best measurement. Complete this test each week and compare your results.

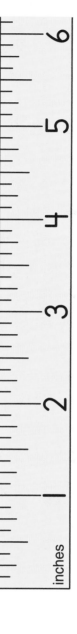

Gather some balls near a sidewalk. Draw a chalk line and stand on it. Throw a ball as far away as you can. Ask a friend to put a stick on the spot where the ball landed. Do this several times, then measure your longest throw.

► **Write the number that comes before, between, or after each number or numbers.**

Before	**Between**	**After**
I. _____ 347	6. 213 _____ 215	II. 679 _____
2. _____ 528	7. 427 _____ 429	12. 721 _____
3. _____ 832	8. 399 _____ 401	13. 398 _____
4. _____ 731	9. 478 _____ 480	14. 599 _____
5. _____ 293	10. 871 _____ 873	15. 734 _____

Write each letter of the alphabet on an index card. Go outside with the cards. Look for something that starts with *A*, such as an acorn. Write acorn on the *A* card. Keep going until you find something for every letter. Look out—some are tricky!

▶ **Write *person*, *place*, or *thing* to identify each underlined noun.**

1. The <u>child</u> ate lunch at noon. _____

2. They went to the <u>park</u> to play soccer. _____

3. The <u>teacher</u> heard the children sing. _____

4. The boys and girls rowed a <u>boat</u>. _____

5. One girl went down the <u>slide</u>. _____

6. Kendra and her dad went to the <u>store</u>. _____

7. <u>Winston</u> planted the pumpkin seeds. _____

8. Nadia's missing <u>shoe</u> was under the sofa. _____

Put newspaper inside an old T-shirt. Ask permission to write on the shirt. Use markers to write your favorite foods, friends, shows, and books on the shirt. Draw pictures if you like. Wear the shirt to tell people all about you.

▶ **Read the passage. Then, answer the questions.**

Helpful Insects and Arachnids

Some insects can destroy crops, such as fruits and vegetables, by eating them. Not all insects are bad, though. Some insects help people. Bees move pollen from flower to flower. This helps flowers make seeds so that there will be more flowers the next year. Bees also produce honey. Ladybugs are helpful insects, too. They eat the insects that chew on plants. Finally, spiders may look scary, but they are helpful. They are not insects. They are arachnids. They catch flies, crickets, and moths in their webs. If you find a spider in your home, ask an adult to help you carefully place it outside. Then, it can do its job.

1. What is the main idea of this passage?

  A. Insects can destroy crops.

  B. Ladybugs are beautiful.

  C. Some insects and arachnids are helpful.

2. How do bees help flowers grow? _____

   _____

3. How are ladybugs helpful?_____

   _____

Some say that fireflies light up to meet other fireflies. Sit outside at dusk. Count the number of fireflies you see for two minutes. Turn on a small flashlight. Count for two more minutes. Did you see more or fewer fireflies?

12

▶ Write > (greater than) or < (less than) to compare each pair of numbers.

1. 2 ◯ 4

2. 124 ◯ 216

3. 19 ◯ 91

4. 592 ◯ 324

5. 14 ◯ 4

6. 322 ◯ 100

7. 9 ◯ 10

8. 985 ◯ 850

9. 64 ◯ 46

10. 648 ◯ 846

11. 29 ◯ 30

12. 745 ◯ 746

Choose a house or building that you like. Look at it for a long time. Turn around and draw a quick sketch of it. Compare your drawing to the building to see what is the same and what is different.

13

► **Write a noun from the word bank to complete each sentence.**

bank	camera	mud
bike	hero	palace

1. The rain turned the dirt into _____ .

2. I took a picture of my family with a _____ .

3. The tires on the _____ needed air.

4. I put the money I saved in a _____ .

5. The _____ of the story was a man who helped people.

6. The king and queen live in a _____ .

Draw a great playground for your yard or park. Add slides, swings, climbing walls, and lots of other great stuff. Be sure to draw children playing on it.

14

▶ **Synonyms** are words that have the same meaning. Read the story. Then, write a synonym from the word bank for each underlined word.

happy	notice	trail
outdoors	run	woods

Jogging with Mom

Mom and I like to <u>jog</u> every evening. We sometimes take our dog, Rudy. We turn down a <u>path</u> and jog through the <u>forest</u>. We <u>see</u> the tall trees and listen to our feet hitting the ground. Being <u>outside</u> at sundown makes me feel <u>joyful</u>.

1. jog _____

2. path _____

3. forest _____

4. see _____

5. outside _____

6. joyful _____

Help birds build nests. Gather yarn, fabric strips, twigs, and newspaper strips. Tie them in a loose bundle. Tie the bundle to a tree branch. Do you see nests in your area that include the goodies you provided?

▶ **Read each word aloud. Listen to the vowel sounds. If the word has a short vowel sound, write S on the line. If the word has a long vowel sound, write L on the line.**

EXAMPLE:

just _____S_____

1. cape _____

2. clock _____

3. cute _____

4. bug _____

5. ship _____

6. nice _____

7. apple _____

8. goat _____

9. road _____

10. help _____

11. read _____

The next time you eat one of your favorite fruits, save some of the seeds. Ask an adult for some small paper cups and fill each cup with dirt. Add seeds and water to each of the cups. Put them in a sunny window. As the plants sprout and grow, plant them outside.

▶ **Find the place value of each underlined digit. Circle the answer.**

EXAMPLE:

8<u>9</u>	**1.** 2<u>9</u>	**2.** <u>1</u>4
9 tens	2 tens	1 ten
(9 ones)	2 ones	1 one

3. 6<u>3</u>	**4.** <u>3</u>8	**5.** 1<u>0</u>
3 tens	3 tens	0 tens
3 ones	3 ones	0 ones

6. <u>4</u>	**7.** <u>7</u>1	**8.** 9<u>9</u>
4 tens	7 tens	9 tens
4 ones	7 ones	9 ones

The next time you visit a friend or family member, make up a song about it. In the song, tell about what you will do while you are there. Write down the words. Sing the song as you travel.

▶ **A proper noun names a specific person, place, or thing. Each word of a proper noun begins with a capital letter. Write the name of each person correctly.**

I. cindy lewis _____

2. nicholas jones _____

3. ms. cohen _____

4. don li _____

5. mr. finley _____

6. ellen garza _____

7. dr. monica seth _____

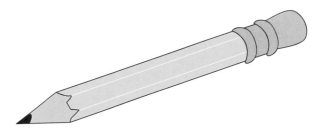

 Hand signals tell where you are going. Hold your left arm straight out to say, "I am turning left." Bend your left arm up to say, "I am turning right." Bend your left arm down to say, "I am stopping." Run around or ride your bike outside and practice the signals.

► **Antonyms** are words that have opposite meanings. Read each sentence. Then, circle the antonym for the underlined word in each sentence.

1. Praise your friends when they do <u>good</u> work.

   bad   funny

2. Mom told me to wear <u>clean</u> clothes.

   dirty   new

3. We should be <u>quiet</u> at the playground.

   soft   noisy

4. The bread I <u>bought</u> last week was old.

   sold   found

5. I rode my <u>new</u> scooter to Hannah's house.

   old   green

Write down the entire name of a street near your home. In ten minutes, see how many words you can make from the letters in the street name. Give yourself a point for each word. Ask a friend to beat your score.

19

▶ **Read each word aloud. Then, write *short* or *long* for each vowel sound.**

1. bug _____

2. cake _____

3. cut _____

4. gum _____

5. road _____

6. catch _____

7. cube _____

8. clock _____

9. stick _____

10. child _____

11. mop _____

12. these _____

13. street _____

14. log _____

15. fly _____

16. boat _____

Pretend you will celebrate a favorite winter holiday in the summer! Draw a picture of the new holiday. What would you wear? What would you eat? What else would change?

▶ **Follow the directions below for each problem.**

1. **Circle the number if 6 is in the hundreds place.**

629	426	47
926	682	26
636	426	660

2. **Circle the number if 9 is in the ones place.**

79	429	609
191	509	94
889	69	209

3. **Circle the number if 3 is in the tens place.**

231	722	38
1,639	63	530
333	32	23

4. **Circle the number if 5 is in the tens place.**

54	151	555
185	250	58
50	725	255

5. **Circle the number if 4 is in the hundreds place.**

1,423	484	124
2,642	1,600	432
3,046	4,422	144

6. **Circle the number if 7 is in the ones place.**

27	147	607
38	78	447
99	997	1,007

Create your own language! Write down a new word for 10 things you see. Share the words with a friend. When you ask your friend to go to the "squenner," only your friend will know you really mean "playground."

▶ **Underline the proper noun in each sentence.**

1. Do you like to visit Jefferson Library?

2. Woodland School is where he will go to school next year.

3. My grandmother lives in France.

4. Roberto's is my favorite restaurant.

5. My cat Fifi likes to sleep all day.

6. Julia is my best friend.

7. Renee shares a computer with her brother.

Pretend that you are trading houses with a friend.
Make a list of fun places that are near your house,
such as the playground and the ice cream shop.
Draw a map to help your friend get there.

► **Read the passage. Then, answer the questions.**

Railroads

Railroads have played an important part in history. For centuries, railroads have helped carry people and goods long distances. In the United States, travel was much harder before a railroad connected the eastern and western parts of the country. Workers in the eastern United States built a railroad heading west. A different crew in the west started building a railroad heading east. In 1869, the two lines met in the state of Utah. The crews hammered in a special golden nail to tie the two tracks together. After that, people could travel easily and quickly from one coast of the United States to the other! The next time you stop at a railroad crossing to let a train pass, think about how important railroads have been in history.

1. What is the main idea of this passage?

   A. Railroads played an important part in history.

   B. No one uses railroads today.

   C. You have to stop to let trains go by.

2. What could people do once the railroad was completed? _____

_____

3. What did the crews use to join the two tracks? _____

_____

Line up some empty plastic bottles on a wall. Stand a few feet away. Throw balls at the bottles and count how many times you throw before you hit all of them. Keep trying until the number of throws goes down.

Read and answer each question.

EXAMPLE:

Circle the digits that are in the tens place.

2,4②1   3②8   ⑥1

5③6   ⑧4   1,6⓪2

1. Circle the digits that are in the thousands place.

7,816   121   6,211

44   729   4,864

2. Circle the digits that are in the ones place.

26   842   463

924   19   846

3. Circle the digits that are in the hundreds place.

481   643   970

1,294   1,122   2,351

4. What does the circled number mean?   51⑥

6 ones   6 tens   6 hundreds

5. What does the circled number mean?   ②64

2 ones   2 tens   2 hundreds

Make a time capsule from a plastic box with a lid. Put in a list of things you like and dislike, your friends' names, and the date. Add some pictures of yourself. Store the box under your bed for a few months. What do you think will be different when you open it?

► **Write each noun and proper noun from the word bank in the correct column.**

April	farmer	man	Mexico City	Ms. Sho
park	Sunny Market	teacher	Thursday	ticket

Noun   **Proper Noun**

_____   _____

_____   _____

_____   _____

_____   _____

_____   _____

Make up a tongue twister. Use the first letter sound of your first name. For example, if your name is Drew, your tongue twister could be, "Drew draws dogs daily." How fast can your friends say it without getting tongue-tied?

▶ **In each box, write the missing number.**

1.
```
      5
+ [   ]
------
     12
```

2.
```
   [   ]
+    3
------
     8
```

3.
```
      7
+ [   ]
------
     16
```

4.
```
      8
+ [   ]
------
     18
```

5.
```
   [   ]
+    2
------
     6
```

6.
```
   [   ]
+    4
------
     10
```

7.
```
   [   ]
+    8
------
     18
```

8.
```
      1
   [   ]
+    4
```

Have an adult take you on a button quest. See how many buttons you can find. Check at crosswalks or in the window of your family car. You may even find a button near your front door.

▶ **Homophones** are words that sound the same but are spelled differently and have different meanings. Write a homophone from the word bank for each underlined word.

bee	new	one	right	wood

1. Did you <u>write</u> the _____ answer?

2. Nathan only <u>won</u> _____ game.

3. <u>Would</u> you cut some _____ for the fireplace?

4. <u>Be</u> careful, or that _____ will sting you!

5. I <u>knew</u> I would get some _____ shoes.

Ask an adult to help you interview a neighbor. Ask how long the neighbor has lived there and what she likes about her home. Write down the answers. Share a copy of the interview with your neighbor.

27

▶ **Think about your favorite holiday. Describe this holiday using each of your five senses. What do you see, hear, feel, smell, and taste?**

_____

_____

_____

_____

_____

_____

_____

_____

_____

_____

Insects and other animals transfer yellow dust called _pollen_ from flower to flower. This helps plants grow fruit. Sit outside and watch some flowers. List all of the animals that land on them.

► **Add or subtract to solve each problem.**

1.   7
    + 2

2.   3
    + 0

3.   8
    + 3

4.   6
    + 2

5.   9
    + 0

6.   3
    − 2

7.   5
    − 0

8.   5
    − 2

9.   10
    − 2

10.   7
    − 3

11.   5
    − 3

12.   6
    + 4

13.   7
    − 2

14.   8
    − 4

15.   2
    + 2

Draw a line down the middle of a piece of paper. On one side, write *nature*. On the other side, write *manmade*. Look up at the sky. Write down everything you see that is part of nature under the *nature* column. Write everything that is manmade in the *manmade* column.

Read each sentence. Listen to the first vowel in the highlighted word. If it is a long vowel sound, circle _long_. If it is a short vowel sound, circle _short_.

1. Ray skied down the **slope**.   long   short

2. I put my picture inside a **frame**.   long   short

3. The **kite** was flying high in the air.   long   short

4. I asked Sean to **toss** the ball to me.   long   short

5. Ann picked a **bunch** of flowers from the field.   long   short

6. Tina is Marie's **sister**.   long   short

7. Put those papers in the **trash**.   long   short

8. I sat on the **bench** in the park.   long   short

9. The **tube** of toothpaste was empty.   long   short

Take a few cotton swabs, some paint, and a sheet of paper outside. Choose an object to paint. Try to make a painting with just dots, without rubbing the swabs on the paper. Can you make the dots look like the object?

▶ **Write each singular or plural noun from the word bank in the correct column.**

fork	guitar
peanut	shirts
crickets	keys
pond	toes

Singular   **Plural**

_____   _____

_____   _____

_____   _____

_____   _____

Stand on a sunny sidewalk. Have a friend make a silly pose. Trace your friend's shadow with chalk, then let your friend trace your shadow. Try to make the same poses and "fit" back into the tracings.

▶ **When a prefix is added to a base word, it changes the meaning of the word. Circle the prefix in each word. Then, write the letter of the correct definition next to the word.**

1. _____ reopen

2. _____ unhappy

3. _____ misplace

4. _____ unsure

5. _____ misuse

6. _____ redo

7. _____ undo

A. to wrongly place

B. not happy

C. to wrongly use

D. to open again

E. to cancel

F. not sure

G. to do again

Gather at least ten rocks and rinse them with water. Group the rocks by size, then by color. Rub the rocks together to find one rock that will scratch all of the others. This is the hardest rock.

Look at each word. Write how many vowels you see. Then, read each word aloud. Write how many vowel sounds you hear.

		Vowels	Vowel Sounds				Vowels	Vowel Sounds
1.	puzzle	_____	_____		9.	radio	_____	_____
2.	cookies	_____	_____		10.	carrot	_____	_____
3.	blocks	_____	_____		11.	sleep	_____	_____
4.	alphabet	_____	_____		12.	wanted	_____	_____
5.	goat	_____	_____		13.	heart	_____	_____
6.	jump	_____	_____		14.	useful	_____	_____
7.	pilot	_____	_____		15.	beautiful	_____	_____
8.	lion	_____	_____		16.	water	_____	_____

Go outside and try to find 20 things that use electricity. Make a list of what you find. Ask an adult to take you to look for things that use electricity at night. Did you find the same things?

▶ **Write the related facts for each fact family.**

1.

_____ + _____ = _____

_____ + _____ = _____

_____ − _____ = _____

_____ − _____ = _____

2.

_____ + _____ = _____

_____ + _____ = _____

_____ − _____ = _____

_____ − _____ = _____

3.

_____ + _____ = _____

_____ + _____ = _____

_____ − _____ = _____

_____ − _____ = _____

It is hard to build a tower in nature. Gather some sticks, rocks, and other objects from outside. Try to use them to build a tower. Keep trying until you find a way to stack all of your objects together.

▶ **Circle the correct word to complete each sentence.**

1. Mark planted a (tree, trees) in his backyard.

2. Sam and his mother bought two (apple, apples) at the grocery store.

3. Andrea fed each dog one (treat, treats).

4. There were three (flag, flags) at the store.

5. All of the (swing, swings) in the park were full.

6. Talia has a new (sister, sisters).

7. I like to draw (picture, pictures).

Veins help move blood around your body. Leaves have veins too. Use a magnifying glass to examine a few leaves. Find the largest vein down the middle and then look for smaller veins. Which leaf has the most veins?

► **When a suffix is added to a base word, it changes the meaning of the word. Add** *-less* **or** *-ness* **to the base word in each sentence.**

EXAMPLE:

The children were very _____rest**less**_____ today.

1. The _____friendli_____ of the people made us feel at home.

2. Trying to train my dog to roll over is _____hope_____ .

3. The baby loves the _____soft_____ of her blanket.

4. The _____loud_____ of the noise made me jump.

5. Her _____happi_____ showed on her face.

Go outside in the daytime and find the moon. If you cannot see it, try later. List as many phrases as you can think of to describe where you see the moon, such as *over my house* and *next to the pine tree*.

► **Read each word in the word bank. If the *y* makes the long *i* sound, as in *fly*, write the word under the fly. If the *y* makes the long *e* sound, as in *city*, write the word under the city scene.**

baby	happy
dry	sky
eye	story

fly

city

_____   _____

_____   _____

_____   _____

The word *terrain* means the land around you. It also means objects that are part of the land. Look around. Try to spot a hill, mountain, cliff, valley, river, pond, lake, stream, ocean, beach, forest, meadow, field, building, road, and bridge.

37

▶ Write the missing sign (+, −, or =) in each number sentence.

1. 6 _____ 3 = 9

2. 12 _____ 6 = 6

3. 4 _____ 2 = 2

4. 4 + 3 _____ 7

5. 14 _____ 1 = 15

6. 12 _____ 2 = 10

7. 9 _____ 3 = 6

8. 14 _____ 4 = 10

9. 14 − 7 _____ 7

10. 4 _____ 1 = 3

11. 7 − 3 _____ 4

12. 3 _____ 3 = 6

13. 8 _____ 4 = 12

14. 9 _____ 2 = 11

15. 11 _____ 2 = 9

Make paper bag animals. Ask for old magazines. Cut out eyes, noses, ears, tails, and other animal parts. Glue them to a paper lunch bag. Mix up the parts to make new, weird animals, then stuff them with newspaper and tape the bags shut.

▶ Circle the word that completes each sentence.

1. Two _____ went for a ride.   girl   girls

2. My _____ broke when it fell.   dish   dishes

3. Which _____ is yours?   pencil   pencils

4. Put all of the _____ back on the shelf.   book   books

5. My foot is nine _____ long.   inch   inches

6. How many _____ were in the race?   boat   boats

7. May I have a piece of _____ ?   pie   pies

8. Where are my_____ ?   shoe   shoes

9. That _____ belongs to Roger.   paper   papers

10. Angelica made a _____ for Sarah.   gift   gifts

Some American Indian tribes perform rain dances. Invent your own weather dance! Make your dance moves match the weather you want. Perform your dance for your family.

▶ **Underline the compound word in each sentence. Then, draw a line between the two word parts.**

EXAMPLE:

Rebecca lives on a <u>house</u>|<u>boat</u>.

1. A raindrop hit the white rabbit on the nose.

2. Let's go visit the lighthouse.

3. Did you hear the doorbell ring?

4. The horses are in the barnyard.

5. I cleaned my bedroom this morning.

6. The snowflakes fell very quickly.

Each kind of spider makes a different kind of web. Take paper and a pencil outside in the morning and look for spider webs. When you find a web, draw it. See how many different kinds of webs you can find.

► **How quickly can you complete this page? Time yourself. Ready, set,** *go!*

1. 9 − 4 = _____

2. 7 − 6 = _____

3. 4 − 4 = _____

4. 3 − 2 = _____

5. 6 − 4 = _____

6. 5 − 5 = _____

7. 8 − 0 = _____

8. 7 − 1 = _____

9. 9 − 8 = _____

10. 2 − 1 = _____

11. 0 − 0 = _____

12. 3 − 1 = _____

13. 8 − 4 = _____

14. 2 − 1 = _____

15. 6 − 2 = _____

16. 5 − 4 = _____

17. 8 − 3 = _____

18. 5 − 1 = _____

19. 8 − 5 = _____

20. 9 − 1 = _____

21. 6 − 1 = _____

22. 5 − 2 = _____

23. 6 − 5 = _____

24. 7 − 2 = _____

Time: _____   Number correct: _____

Dirt is full of rotting leaves, tiny animals, and even tiny bits of metal. Dig up a little dirt. Rub a magnet through it. What happens?

41

▶ Read the paragraph. Then, answer the questions.

Everyone wants to be treated fairly. Being fair means treating others like you want to be treated. Think about a time when you were treated unfairly. How did that make you feel? Read the following situations. Below, write about what you would do in each situation.

- You have two friends who are staying at your house after your party. It is time for a snack, and you each want a leftover cupcake. Only two cupcakes are left. What would you do?

- Your younger sister is learning to play a new board game. She asks you to play it with her. As you play, you see that she gave you an extra card. The card will help you win. What would you do?

_____

_____

_____

_____

_____

_____

Stores arrange things nicely in windows to make people want to buy them. Make your own shop window. Place a table under a window inside of your house. Arrange your favorite toys on the table. Stand back to see how your toys would look to shoppers.

▶ **Change each singular noun to its plural form.**

> A **plural** noun names more than one person, place, or thing.
>
> Most nouns become plural by adding **s**.
> book → book**s**   shirt → shirt**s**
>
> Nouns that end in **s, ch, sh,** or **x** become plural by adding **es**.
> kiss → kiss**es**   branch → branch**es**   wish → wish**es**   ax → ax**es**

I. picture _____   2. peach _____

3. tree _____   4. chair _____

5. dish _____   6. fox _____

▶ **Write a sentence using one of the plural nouns from above.**

7. _____

_____

Grab a paintbrush and some water. Find a clean sidewalk. Dip the paintbrush in the water. "Paint" a picture on the sidewalk. Wait for the water to evaporate. Then, paint something else.

43

▶ **Solve each problem.**

1. Allison had 8 baseballs. She lost 2 of them. How many baseballs does she have left?

2. Liam had 6 apples. He gave 4 apples away. How many apples does Liam have left?

3. Shannon walked 2 miles. Lori walked 3 miles. How many total miles did the children walk?

4. Nassim saw 8 puppies. Joy saw 4 puppies. How many total puppies did the children see?

On a piece of paper, write the words *stripes, dots, plain,* and *plaid.* Go outside and look for these patterns on people's clothing, cars, and buildings. Make a tally mark on your paper next to each pattern as you find it.

▶ **Solve each riddle. Write the correct singular and plural forms.**

1. I am made of paper, and I have a cover. My name rhymes with *look*.

   I am a _____ .

   My plural form is _____ .

2. I am a round, fuzzy, and sweet fruit. My name rhymes with *beach*.

   I am a _____ .

   My plural form is _____ .

3. I can be made of sticks and grass, and birds live in me. My name rhymes with *best*.

   I am a _____ .

   My plural form is _____ .

Do you have a statue in your town? How about a pretend gnome in your garden? Draw a statue you would like to have, then model it out of clay or play dough. Let it dry and place it outside.

▶ **Read each sentence. Then, write the letter of the underlined word's definition.**

EXAMPLE:

___B___   The birds can <u>fly</u>.   A. a small winged insect

___A___   The spider ate the <u>fly</u>.   B. to move through the air

---

1. _____   Please turn on the <u>light</u>.   A. a lamp

_____   The box is <u>light</u>.   B. not heavy

---

2. _____   <u>Store</u> the books on the shelf.   A. a place to buy things

_____   I bought a dress at the <u>store</u>.   B. to put away for the future

---

3. _____   Drop a penny in the <u>well</u>.   A. healthy

_____   Are you feeling <u>well</u>?   B. a hole to access underground water

Find a small hill outside. How many ways can you get down the hill? Try rolling, skipping, walking, and more. When you cannot think of another way to get down the hill, try using all of those ways to get back up the hill.

► **Circle each word that has the /o͞o/ sound, as in** *tooth*. **Draw an X on each word that has the /o͝o/ sound, as in** *hook*.

book	wood	scoop
hood	tool	crook
took	hoop	spoon
moon	pool	cook
school	food	cool
zoo	moose	foot
soon	boot	goose
stool	wool	stood

Got a new book to enjoy? Look around for a new, special book nook where you can enjoy it. Try some unusual reading spaces. Sit on the floor in a corner of a room, on a porch, or outside under a shady tree.

▶ **Fill in the circle beside the correct plural of each word.**

1. glass

many ○ glass
○ glasses

2. paintbrush

several ○ paintbrushs
○ paintbrushes

3. dish

more ○ dishs
○ dishes

4. sandwich

four ○ sandwiches
○ sandwichs

Has it rained lately? If you can find a puddle, you can float a boat. Fold some aluminum foil into a canoe shape. Make sure the bottom is flat. Experiment with different shapes to see which one floats best.

48

▶ **Draw a line to match the problems that have the same sum.**

EXAMPLE:

10 + 3   A. 9 + 2

1. 5 + 6   B. 8 + 8

2. 8 + 4   C. 8 + 5

3. 9 + 7   D. 3 + 6

4. 4 + 5   E. 3 + 7

5. 6 + 4   F. 4 + 2

6. 6 + 9   G. 5 + 13

7. 9 + 8   H. 5 + 9

8. 6 + 0   I. 3 + 9

9. 9 + 9   J. 7 + 8

10. 7 + 7   K. 14 + 3

You never know what you will find under a rock. Take some paper and a pencil outside. Turn over a few rocks or small logs. Write down what scurries away. Put a tally mark next to any critter that you see more than once.

▶ **Complete each sentence by adding the suffix -*ing* to the word in parentheses. When a word ends in *e*, drop the *e* before adding the suffix.**

1. We go ice-_____ on the pond every winter.
   (skate)

2. Tad's jersey was _____ because he wore it so often.
   (fade)

3. My sister is _____ decorations for my birthday party.
   (make)

4. Sean and his family are _____ to Florida this summer.
   (drive)

5. Shannon and Leslie are _____ their bicycles this summer.
   (ride)

6. Because of poor business, the store is _____ permanently.
   (close)

Grab a jump rope. Sing your favorite song. Try to keep jumping rope without stumbling until you finish the song. As you get better, sing longer songs.

► **Change the spelling of each underlined word to make it plural. Use the word bank if you need help.**

feet	geese	knives	leaves	men	mice	teeth

1. more than one <u>man</u> _____

2. more than one <u>tooth</u> _____

3. more than one <u>leaf</u> _____

4. more than one <u>goose</u> _____

5. more than one <u>knife</u> _____

6. more than one <u>mouse</u> _____

7. more than one <u>foot</u> _____

You do not need a partner to play tennis. Pick up a racket and ball and find a wall. The wall should be at least 10 feet high with no windows. Toss the ball in the air and hit it against the wall. See how many times you can hit the ball without missing.

▶ **How quickly can you complete this page? Time yourself. Ready, set,** *go!*

1. 12
   − 4

2. 10
   − 7

3. 11
   − 4

4. 7
   − 5

5. 9
   − 7

6. 11
   − 9

7. 10
   − 2

8. 12
   − 8

9. 9
   − 3

10. 7
    − 3

11. 11
    − 5

12. 12
    − 7

13. 12
    − 3

14. 8
    − 7

15. 9
    − 6

16. 9
    − 2

17. 6
    − 3

18. 10
    − 3

19. 12
    − 9

20. 8
    − 2

Time: _____   Number correct: _____

Catch some colorful bubbles. Add a few drops of food coloring to a bottle of bubble solution. Blow some bubbles outside. Catch them on a white paper plate. You made bubble art! To make another bubble color, add a different color to the bubbles. How can you make brown bubbles?

▶ **Write each word from the word bank under the correct heading.**

shirt	socks	pliers
saw	bear	deer
elephant	screwdriver	hammer
pants	fox	hat

Animals   **Tools**   **Clothing**

_____   _____   _____

_____   _____   _____

_____   _____   _____

_____   _____   _____

Need to get some things done? Make a to-do list like the ones adults make all the time for work and chores. Make yours fun by adding items such as _Play with Jon next door_ and _Eat lunch outside._

► **Write str-, spr-, spl-, or thr- to complete each word.**

1. _____ eet

2. _____ ough

3. _____ ang

4. _____ ash

5. _____ it

6. _____ ow

7. _____ ong

8. _____ ee

9. _____ ay

10. _____ atter

Who needs candy necklaces? Grab some elastic (stretchy) string and your favorite o-shaped cereals. String the cereal onto the string. Tie it around your wrist. Make some crunchy jewelry for your friends too.

▶ **Add to find each sum.**

1. 2
    3
  + 2

2. 4
    4
  + 2

3. 5
    1
  + 1

4. 9
    1
  + 0

5. 7
    2
  + 1

6. 1
    2
  + 6

7. 5
    2
  + 5

8. 6
    1
  + 7

9. 2
    5
  + 4

10. 8
     1
   + 2

11. 2 + 2 + 2 = _____

12. 0 + 0 + 8 = _____

13. 1 + 0 + 8 = _____

14. 5 + 1 + 1 = _____

15. 2 + 5 + 3 = _____

16. 9 + 2 + 2 = _____

Make an anti-boredom list. Pick a letter of the alphabet. List ten things you wish you were doing that start with that letter. Pick the best thing on the list and do it. Save your list for the next time you are bored or make a new one with a new letter.

► **Write _he_, _she_, _it_, or _they_ in place of the underlined word or words.**

1. The computer was a gift to the school.

   _____ was a gift to the school.

2. The Johnsons moved into the house next door.

   _____ moved into the house next door.

3. Dad likes to cook on the weekends.

   _____ likes to cook on the weekends.

4. Clara Barton was a nurse.

   _____ was a nurse.

Here is a funny trick to play on an adult who is reading the newspaper. Hold a paper clip on top of the paper. Tell the adult you are going to make it dance. Secretly move a magnet around on the other side of the paper. Wow, look at that clip dance!

► **Write the correct suffix, -*ing* or -*ed*, on each line.**

1. Bill knock _____ on the door before he went in.

2. I am going fish _____ with my grandfather Saturday.

3. The children toss _____ the ball to each other.

4. Grandmother is dish _____ up the ice cream.

5. Are you still look _____ for your wallet?

6. Tyrone splash _____ me as he jumped into the pond.

Write a letter to someone you miss. Describe something you did or tell a funny story. Put the letter in an envelope. Write the address on the front, add a stamp, and seal the letter. Mail it and see what happens.

57

▶ **Add to solve each problem.**

1.   4
        8
    + 6

2.   5
        2
    + 3

3.   5
        1
    + 7

4.   6
        4
    + 1

5. 3 + 8 + 4 = _____

6. 6 + 5 + 5 = _____

7. 3 + 7 + 3 = _____

8. 2 + 2 + 2 = _____

9. 2 + 4 + 7 = _____

10. 5 + 1 + 1 = _____

Ask an adult for an empty, clean spray bottle
and a large sheet of paper. Tape the paper to an
outside wall. Fill the spray bottle with water and
add some food coloring. Spray the paper to make
some spray art.

▶ **Read the passage. Then, answer the questions.**

Washing Your Hands

Your family and teachers have probably told you many times to wash your hands. You should use warm water and soap. Rub your hands together for as long as it takes to sing the alphabet. Then, sing the song again while you rinse your hands. Soap washes off the germs, which are tiny cells that can make you sick. If you do not wash your hands, you can pass a sickness to a friend. Also, you could spread the germs to your eyes or mouth if you touch them before washing your hands. Always remember to wash your hands!

1. What is the main idea of this passage?

   A. Cells can make you sick.

   B. Rub your hands together.

   C. You should wash your hands.

2. What does soap do? _____

_____

3. What could happen if you do not wash your hands? _____

_____

Stuck inside? You can still play hoops. Crumple ten newspaper balls. Place a laundry basket on the other side of the room. Shoot the balls into the basket. Move farther away from the basket or behind furniture to test yourself.

▶ **Subtract to find each difference.**

1. 14
    − 5

2. 11
    − 4

3. 12
    − 5

4. 15
    − 6

5. 16
    − 8

6. 13
    − 4

7. 14
    − 7

8. 13
    − 5

9. 15
    − 7

10. 17
    − 9

11. 15
    − 8

12. 12
    − 3

13. 18
    − 9

14. 14
    − 6

15. 11
    − 6

Play "Add an Adverb." Say a short, silly sentence, such as, "I ate dirt." Your friend should add a word that tells how she ate it, such as, "I ate dirt quietly." Then, during your turn, add a different adverb, such as, "I ate dirt happily." Take turns until one player cannot think of any more adverbs.

► **Write what or whom each underlined word stands for.**

EXAMPLE:

The boys ran to the park. <u>They</u> ran to the park.

They = _____**boys**_____

1. Carla and I like horses. We ride <u>them</u> every week.

them = _____

2. My aunt called today. <u>She</u> is coming to visit us.

She = _____

3. I have a new bike. <u>It</u> is green.

it = _____

4. I lost my umbrella. <u>It</u> is blue.

It = _____

Make a cool kazoo by folding a piece of waxed paper over the teeth of a small comb. Press your lips lightly against the paper and say, "Ooo!" Can you make the paper vibrate?

► **Follow the directions to draw a picture.**

1. Draw a house and a tree.

2. Color the house red.

3. Draw and color one bird under the tree.

4. Draw a sun. Color it yellow.

Dig up a dinosaur in your house! Grab some play dough or glue, and toothpicks or craft sticks. See if you can put together a dino skeleton. Start with the legs, and then add the body and tail. Let any glue dry before you add another section. What could you use for teeth, horns, or spines?

▶ **Read the sentence pairs. Write an X beside the sentence that happens first.**

1. _____ I planted seeds.

   _____ The flowers grew.

2. _____ Luke started his car.

   _____ Luke drove his car.

3. _____ I put on my shoes.

   _____ I put on my socks.

4. _____ We built a snowman.

   _____ Our snowman melted.

5. _____ I brushed my teeth.

   _____ I put toothpaste on my toothbrush.

6. _____ I climbed into bed.

   _____ I fell asleep.

Go on a pretend safari. Hide some plastic toy animals in your backyard. Make a list of where they are so you do not lose any. Lead a few friends or younger siblings through your yard to look for the animals.

▶ **Solve the problems. Find three answers in a row that match.**

Add			Subtract		
12 + 5	8 + 8	10 + 5	11 − 7	12 − 6	10 − 9
6 + 6	8 + 7	8 + 2	9 − 4	10 − 5	11 − 6
9 + 6	9 + 5	6 + 6	18 − 9	11 − 9	10 − 7

Make a wig just for fun. Cut the foot off an old pair of ladies' hose. Blow up a balloon to the size of your head and stretch the hose over the balloon. Glue on as much yarn as you want. Let it dry completely, then pop the balloon and wear your wig. (Throw away all balloon pieces—they can be dangerous for small children and pets.)

Choose the correct pronoun (*he*, *she*, *it*, *we*, or *they*) to replace the highlighted word(s) in each sentence. Write the pronoun on the line.

1. **That boy** rode his bike across the lawn. _____

2. **My grandmother** tells very interesting stories. _____

3. **The bird** sat on its nest for hours. _____

4. **The roller skates** are very rusty. _____

5. **Karin** has to baby-sit tonight. _____

6. **Joelle and Betsy** went to the movies. _____

7. **The balloons** floated up to the sky. _____

8. **Javier and I** went to the library. _____

Who says ice cubes have to be made of water? Add some juice to ice cube trays, freeze them for at least four hours, then pop them out and add them to drinks. If you add red cubes to a blue drink, what will happen?

▶ **If you had to give away all of the things in your bedroom except for three things, which three things (other than your bed) would you keep? Why?**

_____

_____

_____

_____

_____

_____

_____

_____

_____

Make some stamps. Press bottle caps, sponges, alphabet blocks, soup cans, shells, and other objects into paint. Then, stamp them on paper. What else can you use to stamp?

▶ **Write > (greater than), < (less than), or = (equal to) to compare each expression.**

EXAMPLE:

7 + 7 (<) 15

8 + 6 (=) 14

15 (>) 1 + 9

1. 9 + 7 ( ) 16

13 − 4 ( ) 10

4 + 6 ( ) 9

2. 7 + 9 ( ) 18

17 − 9 ( ) 8

14 − 4 ( ) 10

3. 8 + 9 ( ) 9 + 8

11 − 4 ( ) 6 + 2

16 − 4 ( ) 3 + 10

4. 5 + 8 ( ) 6 + 7

12 − 6 ( ) 6 + 6

10 + 1 ( ) 4 + 7

5. 15 − 5 ( ) 13 − 4

18 − 8 ( ) 8 + 8

11 + 1 ( ) 6 + 6

When you put a seashell to your ear, some people say you can hear the ocean. Will only a seashell work? Try putting an empty soup can, a small box, or a cup over your ear. Do you hear the ocean now?

▶ **Read each sentence. Circle the word or words that each underlined word stands for.**

EXAMPLE:

(Carmella) will be home Friday. I will see <u>her</u> then.

1. The fruit is really good. <u>It</u> tastes sweet.

2. José and Henry ran fast. <u>They</u> won the race.

3. My family and I went on a picnic. <u>We</u> had a good time.

4. Marisa plays the piano. <u>She</u> plays very well.

5. I watered the flowers and put <u>them</u> on the bench.

6. Daniel took the dog inside. <u>He</u> took the cat there too.

If you have a magnet and some paper clips, you can make more magnets. Rub a paper clip over the magnet for a few minutes. Use that paper clip to pick up another. What else can you make into magnets?

▶ **Read the passage. Then, circle the answer that tells what the passage is about.**

Birds

All birds are alike in some ways and different in others. They all have wings, but not all of them fly. Some are tame, and some are wild. Some birds sing. Some talk. Some are gentle. Others are not so gentle. Some birds fly very high and far. Others do not. Some birds are colorful while others are plain.

I. A. Some birds are tame. Others are not.

B. All birds are strange and colorful.

C. Birds are alike and different from each other.

▶ **Draw a picture of your favorite kind of bird in the box below.**

Pepper is scared of soap! Sprinkle some pepper into a shallow dish of water. Add one drop of dish soap. Watch the pepper swim away!

▶ Jellyfish Stretch and Glide

It is time to improve your flexibility! Pretend to be a jellyfish with long tentacles. Move around the room. Imagine that you are gliding through the ocean. Stretch your arms from your shoulders to your wrists. Flex each finger. Move your legs smoothly from your hips to your toes. Move your belly, back, and chest from left to right and front to back. Think about how you are moving. You should be slowly stretching several body parts at once. Add soft music or some ocean sounds as you glide toward better flexibility.

Go on a visual scavenger hunt! Gather all kinds of tiny objects, such as pennies, beads, acorns, pebbles, and wiggly eyes. Glue the objects to a piece of poster board. Hang your artwork in your room.

▶ **Solve each problem.**

1. Kara had 13 flowers. She sold 9 of them. How many flowers does she have left?

2. Alexander can walk 2 miles in one hour. How many miles can he walk in two hours?

3. Michael has 14 toy cars, and Todd has 10 toy cars. How many more cars does Michael have than Todd?

4. Tisha has 9 teddy bears. Brittany has 6 dolls, and Shelby has 3 yo-yos. How many toys do the girls have in all?

It takes a steady hand to thread a needle. Ask an adult to give you a plastic needle and thread. First, twirl the end of the thread. Hold the thread in the hand you use for writing. Hold the needle in the other hand. Then, bring your hands together to put the thread through the tiny eye. Can you do it?

► A **verb** is a word that often describes an action. If a verb is in the present tense, the action is happening now. Write the correct present-tense verb from the word bank to complete each sentence.

finds	listens	rides	spills	works

1. My mom _____ to the radio in the morning.

2. Devon _____ at a store near his house.

3. Uncle Bill _____ the bus to work.

4. Lilly _____ her juice when she is in a hurry.

5. Dad _____ pennies everywhere we go.

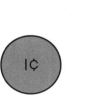 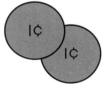

On index cards, write games you love to play, books you want to read, and other activities that you enjoy. Fold the cards and put them in a box with a lid. You made a Fun Box! When you get bored, choose a Fun Card from the box. You HAVE to do what you pick, and you have to have fun!

▶ **Add a subject phrase to complete each sentence.**

1. _____ rode on the Ferris wheel.

2. _____ gave me some money.

3. _____ went to the circus.

4. _____ lifted the heavy weights.

5. _____ did some great magic tricks.

6. _____ bought lots of popcorn.

7. _____ threw the ball.

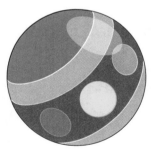

Are ladybugs the same on both sides? Study a ladybug closely with a magnifying glass. Count the number of spots on each side. Does each side have the same number of spots? Are they in the same place?

▶ **Read the passage. Then, answer the questions.**

The Water Cycle

All water on Earth is part of the same cycle. Water starts out in oceans, lakes, and streams. When the sun heats the water, drops of water rise into the air. Water in this form is called water vapor. As the air cools, water droplets form clouds. When the clouds become too heavy with water, they produce rain, sleet, hail, or snow. The water falls back to Earth. Some of the water goes into the soil, where it helps plants grow. Some of the water falls into oceans, lakes, and streams. Then, the water cycle begins again. The next time you drink a glass of water, think about where it came from.

1. What is the main idea of this passage?

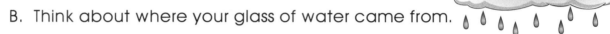

   A. All water on Earth moves through a cycle.

   B. Think about where your glass of water came from.

   C. Rain moves water back to Earth.

2. Where does the water cycle begin? _____

3. When do water droplets form clouds? _____

4. Where does the rain go after it falls back to Earth? _____

_____

You are terrific, so put it down on paper! Make a list of 10 great things about yourself, or 10 things you do well. Tape the list up in your room and read it often. You are the best!

▶ **Add or subtract to solve each problem.**

1. 84
     − 42

2. 37
     − 13

3. 69
     + 20

4. 18
     − 4

5. 57
     + 21

6. 28
     − 16

7. 24
     − 11

8. 10
     − 10

9. 23
     + 12

10. 26
      + 22

11. 43
      + 43

12. 91
      + 6

13. 15
      − 9

14. 12
      + 2

15. 49
      − 38

Ask permission to cut out a few magazine pages with pictures that you like. Glue them to poster board. Let them dry. Cut each picture into 20 pieces. Mix all of the pieces and try to put them back together like a puzzle.

▶ **Circle the present-tense verb in each sentence.**

1. My dog Toby runs fast.

2. Aaron thinks about the question.

3. He goes to class.

4. Angelica paints a picture of flowers.

5. They climb to the top of the mountain.

6. Chad builds snowmen.

7. Jessica and I go to Camp Luna.

8. White clouds float in the blue sky.

9. Chris watches the parade from his window.

10. Jeremy eats lunch at that restaurant.

Take index cards and a pencil outside. Observe people and animals near you. Choose a main character and draw a comic strip about it. Add speech and thought bubbles. Each index card is one panel. Put the cards in order and share your comic with a friend.

▶ **Read the stories. Decide what will happen next. Then, circle the letter beside the answer.**

1. Amy was eating ice cream. Bethany bumped into Amy. What will happen next?

   A. Amy will drink some milk.

   B. Bethany will apologize.

   C. Amy will laugh.

2. Cody was playing tennis with Adam. The sun was very hot. The boys' faces were getting too much sun. What will happen next?

   A. Adam and Cody will go inside.

   B. Cody will walk to the pool.

   C. Cody and Adam will get cold.

Ever get stuck while writing a poem? Make a rhyming list. Go outside to write a nature poem. When you come to a word you want to rhyme, write each letter of the alphabet in a column. Write the word's ending next to each letter. You will soon find a rhyming word that makes sense in your poem.

77

► Together, the letters *ph* make the /*f*/ sound. Read the sentences. Then, write the correct word from the word bank to complete each sentence.

alphabet	amphibian	elephants	phone

1. What is your _____ number?

2. We saw _____ at the zoo.

3. Brad wrote the letters of the _____ .

4. A frog is an _____ .

Missing school? Make a school at home. Arrange a group of stuffed animals or dolls in rows. Teach math, reading, science, and social studies, and give them some homework. Take them to lunch and then outside for recess. Put them all on the bus (your bed) and be the bus driver that takes them home.

▶ Add to find each sum.

1. 324
    + 125

2. 973
    + 24

3. 777
    + 112

4. 206
    + 132

5. 111
    + 88

6. 420
    + 337

7. 623
    + 125

8. 621
    + 126

9. 362
    + 230

10. 175
    + 113

11. 803
    + 104

12. 603
    + 292

13. 600
    + 9

14. 500
    + 300

15. 821
    + 157

Make a machine that rings a bell. Use marbles, dominoes, cardboard tubes, rulers (for ramps), blocks, string, toy cars, and more. Set up the objects. After you roll the marble or knock over the dominoes, a bell should ring at the end. Keep trying!

▶ **If a verb is in the past tense, the action already happened. Add -*ed* or -*d* to a word to show past tense. Add -*ed* when the word ends in a consonant. Add -*d* when the word ends in a vowel.**

EXAMPLE:

wait _____ed_____

1. talk _____

2. clean _____

3. skate_____

4. rain _____

5. wash_____

6. bake_____

7. time _____

8. hope_____

9. look_____

10. laugh _____

11. save _____

12. jump_____

13. work _____

Jazz up a pair of worn-out tennis shoes. Ask permission to glue on buttons, beads, stickers, and more. Take out the laces and color them with markers. Where will you wear your art shoes?

▶ **Read each sentence. Then, answer the questions.**

1. J. T. is going to David's volleyball game.

Who is going to the game? _____

Whose game is it? _____

2. Evan is reading Kendra's book.

Who does the book belong to? _____

Who is reading? _____

Have some extra paper? Make your own paper airplane. Use tape or scissors if you want. Try a few different folds until at least one of your planes can fly. Test all of them. Ready, steady, fly!

81

▶ **Read each sentence. Then, write the correct word from the word bank to complete each sentence.**

quarter	queen	question	quiet	quilt	squeeze

1. _____ the oranges to make juice.

2. I have a colorful _____ on my bed.

3. Shhh, be very_____in the library.

4. The piece of candy cost a _____.

5. The king and the _____ sit on thrones.

6. I would like to ask a_____.

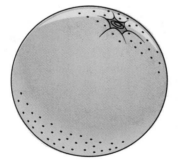

What will happen in the future? Nobody knows, but you can guess. Write a list of ten things you think will happen in the next month. Seal the list in an envelope. One month later, open the envelope. Were your guesses correct?

▶ Subtract to find each difference.

1.   758
      − 126

2.   410
      − 310

3.   894
      − 251

4.   978
      − 165

5.   879
      − 704

6.   785
      − 223

7.   583
      − 161

8.   957
      − 140

9.   683
      − 611

10.   896
       − 840

11.   686
       − 255

12.   349
       − 104

13.   867
       − 36

14.   539
       − 39

15.   767
       − 10

Find a brick building. Count the bricks on one side. Just kidding. You can estimate how many bricks are in the building. Count the rows of bricks from top to bottom, and then across one row. Multiply those two numbers together. The answer is a good estimate of how many bricks there are. How could you estimate the total number of bricks?

▶ **Circle the past-tense verb to complete each sentence.**

1. We (pick, picked) strawberries this morning.

2. I (smile, smiled) when I saw my friend.

3. Maria (search, searched) for her pencil.

4. She (rode, ride) the bus to school.

5. I (ask, asked) Dad if I could go to the museum.

6. Grandma (mend, mended) the tear in my shirt.

7. We (mix, mixed) oil and vinegar to dress the salad.

How can you spend money but keep the coins forever? Make a paper coin collection. Place some coins on a table. Cover them with a sheet of paper. Rub over the paper with the side of a crayon, one coin at a time, to make your paper coin collection. Then, drop the money in a piggy bank.

▶ **Read the poem. Then, answer the questions.**

My Shadow

I have a little shadow that goes in and out with me,
And what can be the use of him is more than I can see.
He is very, very like me from the heels up to the head;
And I see him jump before me, when I jump into my bed.

– Robert Louis Stevenson

1. What does the boy's shadow do when he jumps into bed? _____

_____

2. Who does the boy's shadow look like? _____

3. Where does the boy's shadow go? _____

_____

4. When do you see your shadow? _____

_____

If you have scattered your toys far and wide, go on a clean-up quest! Start in a messy room. Put things that belong in other rooms into an empty basket. Carry the basket to other rooms. Put items away until the basket is empty.

▶ **Read each word. Then, circle the letter or letters that are silent.**

1. (w)rist

2. thum(b)

3. (k)nee

4. (k)not

5. (k)nig(h)t

6. com(b)

7. (k)nife

8. lam(b)

9. si(g)n

10. s(w)ord

11. hig(h)

12. (w)rite

13. (k)now

14. sig(h)

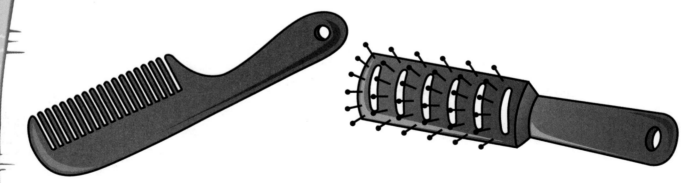

Have a day of doll beauty. Take dolls and action figures outside with a tub of soapy water, a washcloth, and a brush and comb. With adult help, wash their faces and hands, and brush their hair. Wash their clothes if you can. Ah, much better.

Add or subtract to solve each problem.

1. 573
    − 132

2. 832
    + 23

3. 210
    + 153

4. 637
    − 224

5. 638
    − 532

6. 34
    + 25

7. 263
    + 13

8. 508
    − 305

9. 337
    + 231

10. 544
    + 234

11. 872
    + 121

12. 684
    + 102

13. 912
    + 87

14. 500
    + 400

15. 505
    + 292

Jam along with a favorite song. Crank up the music. Grab wooden spoons and metal pots or plastic bowls, and be a terrific drummer. Or, pick up a paper towel tube and sing along. What other instruments do you want to play?

► **Write each verb on the correct ladder.**

blew	find	flew	knew	laugh	wear	~~write~~
blow	found	fly	know	laughed	wore	~~wrote~~

EXAMPLE:

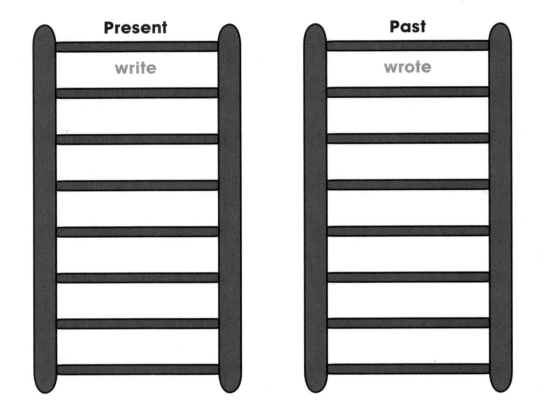

Present

write

Past

wrote

Plan a letter snack. Choose a letter and make a healthy snack that contains only items beginning with that letter. For example, if you chose the letter *a*, you could eat some apricots and apple juice.

88

► **Read each sentence. Write R if the sentence tells something that is real. Write F if the sentence tells something that is a fantasy.**

1. _____ Jennifer wears a watch on her nose.

2. _____ A robin flew to the branch in the tree.

3. _____ Roberto helped his father paint the fence.

4. _____ Danielle heard two trees talking.

5. _____ Kyle eats his lunch with a hammer and a saw.

6. _____ Kayla has two pillows on her bed.

7. _____ Birds use their beaks to fly.

8. _____ Derek lost a baby tooth last night.

9. _____ That cow is driving a bus!

10. _____ The moose gave the frog a cookie.

If you spot a dark, mysterious hole in the ground, write a story about it. Describe what lives in the hole. Did you shrink so that you could explore the hole? Or, did something come out to see you?

89

► Imagine that you are designing a T-shirt for a sports team, a school club, or a special event. Then, draw and color your shirt in the box below. Write a paragraph about your shirt.

It has been said that if you stretch out your arms, they are as long as your body is tall. Ask a friend to measure your arms outstretched, and then measure your height. Are they the same?

▶ **The Impossible Balloon**
Can you inflate a balloon in a bottle?

Materials:
- balloon
- plastic bottle (2-liter)

Procedure:

With an adult, put the balloon inside the bottle while holding on to the mouth of the balloon. Stretch the mouth of the balloon over the mouth of the bottle so that it stays in place. Then, put your lips on the bottle. Try to inflate the balloon.

What's This All About?

When you stretch the balloon over the mouth of the bottle, it seals the bottle. No air can get in or out of the bottle. As you try to inflate the balloon, it pushes against the air inside the bottle. The air pushes on the balloon and does not let the balloon get any bigger. Air takes up space and can push things that push it.

More Fun Ideas to Try:
- Try different sizes of bottles to see if you can inflate the balloon in other bottles.
- Try round balloons or long balloons. Before you try the experiment, write what you think might happen.
- Have an adult punch a small hole in the bottom of a bottle. Try the experiment with this bottle.

Make silly sentences. Go outside and write a sentence about the first animal you see. For example, write *A squirrel lives in a tree.* Think of another animal and then write a sentence such as *A bird lives in a tree and flies.* Keep the list going as long as you can.

Draw a line to connect the subject and predicate phrases in each set to form sentences that make sense.

1. The strong winds   A. uprooted three trees.

2. Our class   B. decoded the message.

3. The spy   C. will visit the fire station.

4. My little brother   D. have fun in art class.

5. The bumblebee   E. fell off his skateboard.

6. We   F. stung my sister.

Create a picture clue game. Cut out about 20 pictures of people from magazines. Place them on a table. On an index card, write a clue for each, such as *She has on a big necklace* or *He is riding a horse.* Mix up the cards. Let a friend try to match the clue cards with their pictures.

► **Follow the directions to find the treasure. Draw an X where the treasure is buried. Then, answer the question.**

- Start in the Red River Valley.
- Go northeast through Lake Lavender to the Black Forest.
- Go northeast to the Evergreen Forest.
- Travel north to the Purple Mountains.
- Cross the Red River to the Blue Mountains.
- Go south, but do not cross the Red River again.
- The treasure is buried here.

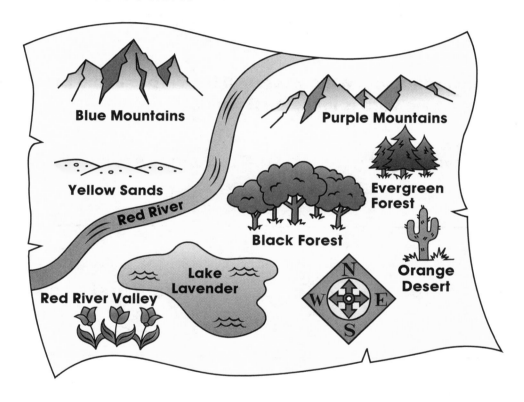

Where is the treasure buried? _____

Hit a plate—win a prize! Get an adult to help you fill a wading pool with water. Float plastic plates on the water, and put a small prize on each plate. Swirl the water to move the plates, then take turns tossing dimes at the plates. Keep the prize you land on—and the dime.

A present tense verb tells about action that is happening now.

It also tells about things that happen often or on a regular basis.

I **walk** home. Sandy **bakes** cookies for Christmas.

A past tense verb tells about action that has already happened.

The letters **ed** or **d** are usually added to change a verb to the past tense.

I **walked** home. I **baked** cookies yesterday.

▶ **Read each sentence. Write** *present* **if the verb is in the present tense. Write** *past* **if the verb is in the past tense.**

1. We played a game.

_____

2. She twirls her hair.

_____

3. I like noodles.

_____

4. Amy talked to me.

_____

Look, no hands! Wipe the end of your nose with a tissue to make it less slippery. Then, breathe on the round end of a metal spoon. Very gently place the spoon over the end of your nose and slowly release it until it hangs from your nose.

▶ A **map key** tells what the symbols on a map stand for. Use the map key to find the objects listed.

1. Circle each city.
2. Draw a square around each baseball park.
3. Draw an X on the state capital.
4. Draw a triangle around the airport.
5. Underline the parks.
6. Draw a star on each university.

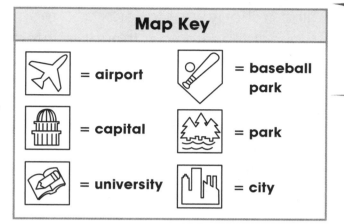

Map Key

✈	= airport	⚾	= baseball park
🏛	= capital	🏞	= park
📖	= university	🏙	= city

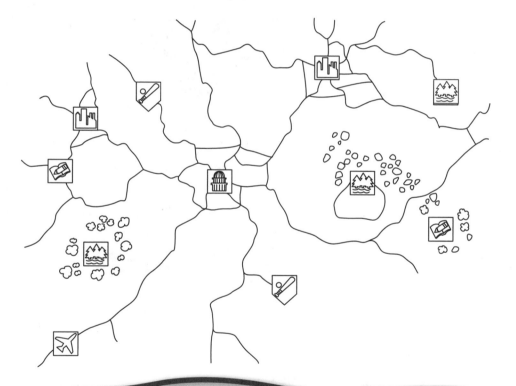

Try drawing abstract art. Choose some crayons. Try sky blue, leaf green, grass green, sunny yellow, or other colors you can see outside. Scribble an abstract drawing. Does your picture feel and look like outside?

▶ Take It Outside!

Summer is a great time to read outdoors. Choose a favorite book and find a shady spot to relax and read. Bring a pencil and notebook too. As you read, write your thoughts, interesting facts, and any new words that you learn. Review your notes at the end of the summer.

Plant a garden! Ask an adult to help you find a large container or choose a spot in the yard. With an adult, go online or visit the library to learn about plants that grow well in your region. Get seeds (vegetable, flower, or herb), some good soil, and water. Plant the seeds. Then, tend your garden by watering and weeding as needed. Record what you planted and when you planted it so that you can chart the growth of your plants. By the end of summer, you will have a garden to be proud of!

It's great to reuse! Ask an adult if you can cut up cards you received during a recent holiday. Cut the fronts off the cards. Make a collage by gluing them to poster board. Glue ribbon around the edge of the board and save it until next year's holiday.

Brent has a street map to help him find his way around his new town. A street map shows where businesses, homes, and other places are located. Look at the street map and answer the questions.

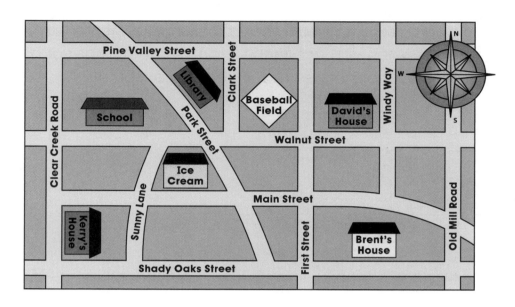

1. Brent lives on _____.

2. David lives at the corner of Walnut Street and _____.

3. The school is on_____.

4. What two streets could Brent take to get to the library?

_____

Photograph each side of your house. Stand the same distance away each time. Glue the pictures to heavy paper and cut them out. Tape the sides together. Fold in the roof, if it is pointed, and tape it together. Can you build your house?

▶ Take It Outside!

Head outside with this page and a pencil. For five minutes, observe what is happening around you. Make a list of the actions you observe, such as a dog barking, a bird flying, a grasshopper jumping, or a person talking. When you are finished, count the number of different verbs on your list. There are so many verbs to observe!

_____

_____

_____

_____

_____

_____

_____

Sometimes when players score in games, they do a victory dance. Make up a victory dance. Do it when you win. Or, just do the dance when something great happens.

▶ Add to find each sum. Add the numbers in the ones place first and carry the number in the tens place from that answer to the box. Then add the numbers in the tens place.

EXAMPLE:

1				
63	**1.** 47	**2.** 19	**3.** 55	**4.** 24
+ 8	+ 8	+ 8	+ 9	+ 7
7 1				

5. 64	**6.** 72	**7.** 48	**8.** 37	**9.** 27
+ 8	+ 8	+ 4	+ 5	+ 6

10. 16	**11.** 33	**12.** 46	**13.** 19	**14.** 28
+ 4	+ 8	+ 8	+ 9	+ 7

Cookie cutters can help you make great coloring books. Put some cookie cutters on a large sheet of paper. Trace around them with a marker. Add details in marker. Then, color them with crayons.

▶ **Draw a line to match each present-tense verb with its past-tense form.**

1. sleep   A. held

2. hold   B. fell

3. make   C. left

4. win   D. bought

5. leave   E. slept

6. fall   F. made

7. buy   G. won

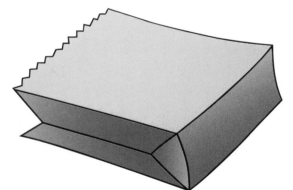

Make a noise maker. Fold down the top of a paper lunch bag. Grip it under the fold and blow it up like a balloon. Squeeze tightly to keep the air in, then smack the bag hard with your other hand.

► **Record how many vowels, syllables, and vowel sounds are in each word. Remember: there are as many syllables in a word as there are vowel sounds.**

△ = number of vowels

☐ = number of syllables

○ = number of vowel sounds

EXAMPLE:

goat △ 2 ☐ 1 ○ 1

1. mailbox △ ☐ ○

2. potato △ ☐ ○

3. dentist △ ☐ ○

4. giant △ ☐ ○

5. tree △ ☐ ○

6. umbrella △ ☐ ○

7. sandbox △ ☐ ○

Here's a fun trick to have up your sleeve. Wrap a rubber band around one end of a small cardboard tube. Stuff the tube with yarn, but leave one end hanging out, and tuck the other end into the rubber band. Tape the tube to your arm. Put on a loose, long-sleeved shirt that matches the yarn. Start pulling the yarn and say, "I think my shirt has a loose string!"

► **Read the sentences. Look at each underlined word. Then, color in the circle to tell if the word is spelled correctly or incorrectly.**

EXAMPLE: **CORRECT**   **INCORRECT**

We <u>ate</u> toast with jam on it.   ●   ○

1. We <u>wint</u> to the store for some bread and milk.   ○   ○

2. The dog will hunt for his <u>boone</u>.   ○   ○

3. We will <u>plant</u> our garden.   ○   ○

4. The <u>keng</u> asked the queen to dance.   ○   ○

5. <u>Think</u> of a good name for a cat.   ○   ○

Make a grass whistle. Make two fists. Put your thumbs together, face-up. Slide a blade of grass between them. Clasp your hands, put your lips on your thumbs, and blow hard. Wiggle the grass around and keep blowing until you hear a loud whistle.

▶ **Subtract to find each difference. Subtract the numbers in the ones place first, borrowing from the tens place if you need to. Then, subract the numbers in the tens place.**

EXAMPLE:

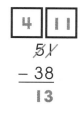

$$\begin{array}{r} 5\cancel{1} \\ -\ 38 \\ \hline 13 \end{array}$$

1. $$\begin{array}{r} 75 \\ -\ 26 \\ \hline \end{array}$$

2. $$\begin{array}{r} 82 \\ -\ 37 \\ \hline \end{array}$$

3. $$\begin{array}{r} 27 \\ -\ 19 \\ \hline \end{array}$$

4. $$\begin{array}{r} 65 \\ -\ 9 \\ \hline \end{array}$$

5. $$\begin{array}{r} 83 \\ -\ 24 \\ \hline \end{array}$$

6. $$\begin{array}{r} 95 \\ -\ 78 \\ \hline \end{array}$$

7. $$\begin{array}{r} 56 \\ -\ 17 \\ \hline \end{array}$$

8. $$\begin{array}{r} 81 \\ -\ 6 \\ \hline \end{array}$$

9. $$\begin{array}{r} 54 \\ -\ 39 \\ \hline \end{array}$$

10. $$\begin{array}{r} 64 \\ -\ 18 \\ \hline \end{array}$$

11. $$\begin{array}{r} 35 \\ -\ 16 \\ \hline \end{array}$$

If you have a stopwatch, you can time yourself doing almost anything. How long does it take to put on your shoes or clean your room? How about walking from one end of your street to the other? Is it always good to do things as fast as you can?

▶ **Write the past-tense form of each verb to complete each sentence.**

1. Chang _____ a card for Alfonso.
   (make)

2. Lindsey_____ her cat to the vet.
   (take)

3. She _____enough bread for a week.
   (buy)

4. Claire and I _____ the movie last night.
   (see)

5. I _____to the gas station.
   (go)

6. The bird _____to the nest.
   (fly)

Do you have a lucky number? See just how lucky you might be. Take a walk to look for your lucky number. Search houses, signs, and vehicles. Make a tally mark on a sheet of paper every time you find it.

▶ **Read the poem. Then, answer the questions.**

Sing a Song of Summer

Sing a song of summer
with arms stretched open wide.
Run in the sunshine.
Play all day outside.

Hold on to the summer
as long as you may.
Autumn will come quickly
and shorten the day.

Play in the water.
Roll in the grass.
It won't be long now
before you'll be in class.

1. Which sentence tells the main idea of the poem?

    A. Enjoy summer while it lasts.   B. Summer gets too hot.

    C. School starts in the autumn.   D. It is fun to sing songs.

2. Write an X beside each thing you can do in the summer.

_____ play outside   _____ rake leaves

_____ go swimming   _____ build a snowman

Every day can be a party. You just have to think of a reason. Declare a holiday for any reason you like. Do some fun activities. Happy _____ Day!

▶ **Add or subtract to solve each problem.**

1.   33
   + 18

2.   62
   − 28

3.   20
   + 19

4.   53
   − 5

5.   58
   + 24

6.   44
   − 18

7.   34
   − 9

8.   72
   + 9

9.   75
   − 47

10.   81
    + 11

11.   31
    − 21

12.   28
    + 14

13.   46
    − 6

14.   31
    − 16

15.   54
    + 27

16.   62
    − 34

Search your kitchen for the perfect snacks. Use crackers, cereal, small candies, nuts, raisins, dried fruit, pretzels, popcorn, and mini marshmallows. Add $\frac{1}{4}$ cup of each to a bowl. Stir and eat. Store leftovers in a plastic box with a lid.

▶ **Write am, is, or are to complete each sentence.**

1. I _____ the tallest girl on the team.

2. My lunch _____ in my backpack.

3. We _____ in line for the roller coaster.

4. I _____ ready to go swimming.

5. Jonah's friends _____ laughing at a joke.

6. Aunt Ebony _____ listening to music.

7. We _____ painting the room blue.

Play this remake of hopscotch. Draw a big square on a driveway. Draw lines to divide it into nine smaller squares. Write 1–9 in the squares in any order. Roll a die and hop on that number, then keep hopping on the numbers in order. For example, if you roll a 3, hop on the 3, and then hop on squares 4–9. If you succeed, give yourself a point.

▶ **Write a synonym from the word bank to take the place of the underlined word in each sentence.**

creek	leaped	middle
largest	giggling	yell

1. He <u>jumped</u> over the mud puddle. _____

2. Let's clap and <u>shout</u> for our team. _____

3. Were the children <u>laughing</u>? _____

4. He is riding the <u>biggest</u> bike. _____

5. We saw fish in the <u>stream</u>. _____

6. Stand in the <u>center</u> of the circle. _____

Good deeds make the doer feel great. Look around your neighborhood for good deeds you could do. You could pick up litter, help a neighbor carry in grocery bags, or bring in someone's paper. What is your good deed for the day?

▶ **Monkeying Around**

With an adult, visit a playground. Find the monkey bars. Begin by swinging by your arms from bar to bar. If you need practice, set a goal such as swing across, rest, and go back. If you are very good at swinging across the bars, see how many times you can go back and forth. You are not just monkeying around! You are improving your upper body strength!

Searching for a way to decide who gets to go first in a game? Try flipping a coin. Play Rock, Paper, Scissors, or Odds and Evens. Can you create your own way to decide who goes first?

▶ **Add to find each sum.**

EXAMPLE:

1

```
   32
   11
 + 19
   62
```

1.
```
   28
   14
 +  4
```

2.
```
   70
   99
 + 12
```

3.
```
   44
    2
 + 38
```

4.
```
   57
   32
 + 89
```

5.
```
   81
   38
 + 64
```

6.
```
   22
    9
 + 19
```

7.
```
   67
   45
 + 15
```

8.
```
   74
   33
 + 17
```

Make grocery shopping fun! Play Guess the Price. At the store, ask an adult to cover the price of an item. Guess its price. How close is your guess? Keep playing with other items. What is your closest guess?

▶ **Write *am*, *is*, or *are* to complete each sentence.**

1. I _____ going to the library.

2. You _____ running to Anton's house.

3. I _____ playing my favorite game.

4. Mom_____sitting in the front row.

5. You _____ the winner!

6. I _____ looking at the ocean.

7. Juan _____ trying to catch a baseball.

8. The rabbit's fur _____ soft.

9. The clothes _____ on sale.

Can you predict the weather? If you look up and see low, thick clouds, then it may rain. If you see wispy, thin clouds high in the sky, the weather may be changing. If you see big, puffy clouds, it may storm later. So, what will your weather be like today?

111

▶ Write the words under the correct heading.

	Synonyms (same)	Antonyms (opposite)	Homophones (sound alike)
Example: would, wood			would, wood
1. high, low			
2. pile, heap			
3. weight, wait			
4. blend, mix			
5. empty, full			
6. rain, reign			
7. cool, warm			

Can you shoot a marble? Place one marble on the ground. Cup another marble in your index finger. Point your hand at the first marble. Tuck your thumb behind the marble and give it a good, hard flick. Try to hit the other marble and make it move while yours stays mostly still.

Use a red pencil to check the problems. Write a ✔ beside each correct answer. Write an X beside each incorrect answer.

1. 423
    + 138
    561

2. 784
    − 107
    618

3. 434
    + 128
    562

4. 324
    + 267
    592

5.   38
    + 19
    57

6. 667
    − 419
    247

7. 410
    − 125
    305

8. 948
    − 819
    129

9. 546
    − 317
    218

10. 634
    − 571
    63

11. 342
    − 237
    105

12. 467
    + 161
    628

13. 861
    − 671
    210

14. 933
    − 673
    260

15. 429
    + 364
    893

16. 685
    + 234
    819

You are a well-known mask maker who is creating a mask using a paper plate. How will you turn the paper plate into a great-looking mask? Make a plan and then make the mask. Share the finished mask with family and friends. Do they like your design?

▶ Unscramble the words to complete each sentence.

Matter is what things are made of. It has three forms:

_____, _____, and _____.
　　(sga)　　　　　　　　　(osdil)　　　　　　　　　　(dqiiul)

_____ can be big or little and soft or hard.
　　(tertaM)

Ice is a _____ . When it melts, it is a _____ .
　　　　　　(dliso)　　　　　　　　　　　　　　　　　　　(ildqui)

_____ is all around you, but you cannot see it.
　　(asG)

Make an amazing strip of paper. Cut a one-inch-wide strip of paper that is about 15 inches long. Turn one end of the strip over, then tape the ends together. This is a Möbius strip. It has only one side. Prove this by drawing a line down one side. When you finish, which side is blank?

▶ **Write *has* or *have* to complete each sentence.**

1. We _____ fun plans for this summer.

2. My mom _____ Friday off.

3. My dad _____ a new book.

4. The girl _____ a hat.

5. Lia and I _____ fruit in our lunches.

6. The doghouses _____ new roofs.

7. His sister _____ dance shoes.

8. The club _____ many members.

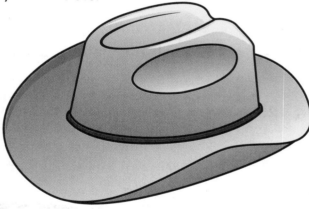

True fans always cheer for their favorite teams. If you have a favorite team, make up a cheer that rhymes. Include clapping and invent some dance moves. Perform the cheer at a game. Go team!

▶ **Read the passage. Then, answer the questions.**

Mercer Mayer

Mercer Mayer's books can be found in many libraries and bookstores. He has both written and illustrated books. Some of his most popular books include *There's a Nightmare in My Closet*; *Liza Lou and the Yeller Belly Swamp*; *Just for You*; and *A Boy, a Dog, and a Frog*. He likes to write about things that happened to him as a child.

Mercer Mayer was born on December 30, 1943, in Arkansas. When he was 13, he moved to Hawaii with his family. After high school, he studied art. Then, he worked for an advertising company in New York. He published his first book in 1967. He and his wife work together on the Little Critter stories. Now, he works from his home in Connecticut.

1. This passage is called a biography. Based on what you read, what do you think a biography is?

   A. a made-up story about a character from a book

   B. a true story that tells about the life of a real person

   C. a short, funny story

▶ **Write *T* for statements that are true. Write *F* for statements that are false.**

2. _____ Mercer Mayer is a character in a book.

3. _____ Mercer Mayer writes about things that happened to him as a child.

People who act out a story without speaking are called *mimes.* Pretend you are a mime trapped inside a glass box. Put your hands flat on the sides of the box to show that you are trapped, since you cannot tell anyone. Then, silently plan your escape.

▶ **Write the time shown on each clock.**

1.

___ : ___

2.

___ : ___

3.

___ : ___

4.

___ : ___

5.

___ : ___

6.

___ : ___

Cool off from your summer quest with water tag. Give a cup of water to one friend, who is "it." Fill a large bucket to be home base. When you say go, "it" should run around and try to tag someone with water. She can refill as often as she likes. The first person to be soaked is the next "it."

117

© Rainbow Bridge Publishing

▶ **The suffix -*ing* is added to a verb to show that something is happening now. Read each word. Then, add -*ing* to the word.**

Example:

go _____going_____

1. say_____

2. do _____

3. sleep_____

4. walk _____

5. read _____

6. paint_____

7. work _____

8. eat _____

9. spell _____

10. cook_____

11. watch_____

Create a new alphabet song. Can you change the tune and still fit all of the letters into the song? Sing your new song for your family.

▶ **Add the prefix *un-* or *re-* to each word. Then, write the meaning of each new word.**

1. sure _____

_____

_____

2. happy _____

_____

_____

3. like _____

_____

_____

4. write _____

_____

_____

5. tell _____

_____

_____

6. print _____

_____

_____

Grab some crayons and paper. Next, play your favorite music. Draw how the music makes you feel. What colors do you feel like? Does the music make you think of a particular image? Now, play a different kind of music. Does the different music make you feel differently? Compare your two pictures.

► **Which character from a book that you have read is most like you? How are you and this character alike?**

_____

_____

_____

_____

_____

_____

_____

_____

Humpty Dumpty had a great fall—ouch! Can you find a way to drop an egg off of a wall without breaking it? Think about how to cushion the egg. Should you wrap it in something? Drop it into something soft? Ask an adult for permission and a couple of eggs, then experiment. Will Humpty make it through this time?

Draw hands on each clock to show the correct time.

1.

12:45

2.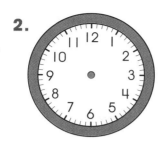

9:15

3.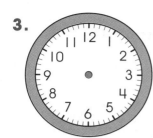

12:30

4.

8:25

5.

5:40

6.

12:05

Look at your reflection in the back of a spoon. See the big nose you have? Now, turn over the spoon. Did gravity reverse itself? Nope, but the light waves reflecting off of the spoon did. Now do you know how funhouse mirrors work?

121

▶ **Add the suffixes *-ed* and *-ing* to each base word. You may need to drop letters from or add letters to some words before adding the suffixes.**

Example:

rake

1. jump

2. hug

_____ raked _____

_____

_____

_____ raking _____

_____

_____

3. cook

4. skate

5. wrap

.

_____

_____

_____

_____

_____

_____

6. sneeze

7. pop

8. talk

_____

_____

_____

_____

_____

_____

How do you know when you see a landmark? When you think, "Oh, now I know where I am." Go for a walk or a drive with an adult and draw your favorite landmarks.

Draw hands on the clock to show what time it is.

1.

2:00

2.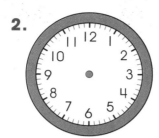

2:15

3.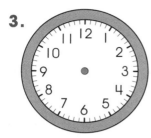

2:30

4.

2:45

5.

2:50

6.

3:00

Amaze your friends by tying water in a knot. Punch three holes in an empty milk carton. They should be in a straight line with about half an inch between each hole. Fill the carton with water. As the water runs out, pinch the three streams together. Ta-dah! A water knot is made.

▶ **Write the letter of the correct definition next to each word.**

1. _____ cheerful   A. ready to help

2. _____ sleepless   B. without sun

3. _____ colorful   C. very cheery

4. _____ sunless   D. having many colors

5. _____ helpful   E. not able to sleep

Make a list of ten exercises, such as stretching, sit-ups, and jumping jacks. Take a pair of dice outside. Roll them and add the numbers. Do that number of the first exercise on your list. Repeat for the rest. When you finish, you should be ready to take a rest!

Look at the map and map key to answer the questions.

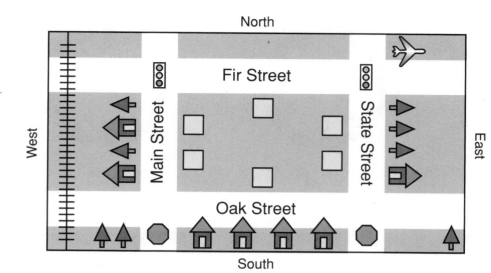

1. The railroad tracks are _____ of Main Street.

   A. north   B. south   C. east   D. west

2. The airport is _____ of State Street.

   A. north   B. south   C. east   D. west

You can make a puppet show! Grab some small markers, a shoebox, and some craft sticks. Draw faces on the craft sticks, then add hair and clothing. Put the shoebox on a table. Squat behind the table and move your tiny actors behind the shoebox. Bravo!

► **Draw hands on each clock to show the correct time.**

1.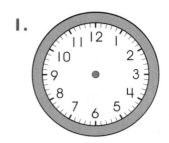

9:25

2.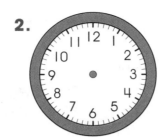

5:05

3.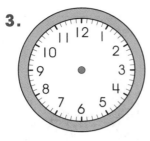

6:35

4.

4:50

 one hour later

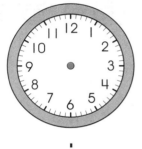

_____:_____

5.

11:10

one hour later

_____:_____

The next time you eat a bowl of cereal, estimate the number of spoonfuls it will take you to eat the entire bowl. Write your estimation down. Now, eat your cereal and make a tally mark for each spoonful you take. When you finish, count the total number of tally marks. How close was your estimation?

Write the word *went* or *gone* to complete each sentence. Remember: the word *gone* needs another word to help it, such as *has* or *have*.

1. Ben _____ home after school.

2. Jessi has _____ shopping for a new coat.

3. Deanna _____ with Andrew to play.

4. We will be _____ on vacation all week.

5. My mother _____ to work this morning.

You do not have to go anywhere to camp. Take an old blanket outside. Turn two chairs back-to-back. Space them far enough apart for you to get between them. Toss the blanket over the chairs and crawl underneath. Ah, relaxing!

▶ Read the passage. Then, answer the questions.

Nightly Navigators

Bats help people in many ways. Most bats eat insects at night. This helps to keep the number of insects low. Bats eat mosquitoes, mayflies, and moths. Bats also pollinate and spread the seeds of many tropical trees.

Bats are the only flying mammals on Earth. There are more than 900 kinds of bats. Some bats are only 1.3 inches (3.3 centimeters) long. Some are more than 16 inches (40 centimeters) long. Most bats eat only insects. Some bats eat fruit and the nectar of flowers.

1. How many different kinds of bats are there? _____

2. What do bats eat? _____

3. How large can some types of bats grow? _____

4. Write three ways that bats help people. _____

   _____

5. Name three types of insects that bats eat. _____

   _____

Be prepared! Ask an adult to help you make an emergency list. At the top, write your home phone number and address. Add 911 for fire and police. List the poison control number and your doctor's office. Be sure to include family phone numbers too. Post the list by the phone.

Complete each sentence by adding your own predicate phrase.

1. The bank robber _____ .

2. Three bluebirds _____ .

3. The quacking duck _____ .

4. The heavy rains _____ .

5. Bill's birthday party _____ .

6. My brother Greg _____ .

7. A brown bear _____ .

8. Thirty-eight clowns _____ .

Give a dramatic reading. Choose a favorite book and find your favorite chapter. Read aloud in a clear voice. Use a different voice for each character. Ask a few friends to choose their favorite books. Sit in a circle and share the readings.

▶ **Circle the coins to equal each amount shown.**

1. 34¢ (10¢) (10¢) (5¢) (5¢) (1¢) (1¢) (1¢) (1¢) (1¢) (1¢)

2. 72¢ (10¢) (10¢) (10¢) (10¢) (10¢) (10¢) (10¢) (1¢) (1¢)

3. 25¢ (5¢) (5¢) (5¢) (5¢) (5¢) (5¢) (1¢) (1¢)

4. 49¢ (10¢) (10¢) (10¢) (10¢) (5¢) (1¢) (1¢) (1¢) (1¢)

Take the dog for a walk—yo-yo style. Slip on a yo-yo string and flick the yo-yo toward the floor. Be careful not to jerk it back up too quickly. Let your yo-yo land gently on the ground and "walk" along the floor, then snap it back up. Good dog!

Write a word from each box to complete each sentence.

1. The train will _____.

   The train is _____.

   The train has _____.

stop
stopped
stopping

2. The baby can _____.

   The baby is _____.

   The baby _____.

clap
clapped
clapping

3. The rabbit is _____.

   The rabbit _____.

   The rabbit can _____.

hop
hopped
hopping

Like bananas? Then open one the "correct" way. Pinch the bottom until it splits, and then pull the peel apart in two nice, neat pieces.

▶ **Write a compound word from the word bank to complete each sentence.**

barefoot	classmates	dinnertime	seashells	springtime

1. Jordan is one of my favorite _____ .

2. Josh likes to walk _____ .

3. It rains a lot during _____ .

4. Our family ate spaghetti at _____ .

5. I like to collect _____ at the beach.

Go on a quest for loose change! Find a large jar to hold the money. Check under couch cushions, on top of dressers, and in the car for loose change. Have an adult pick up some paper coin rolls at the bank. Stack and roll all of the loose change. How much money did you find?

Draw hands on each clock to show the correct time.

1.

   4:50

2.

   7:35

3.

   11:10

4.

   9:25

5. Ellen gets home at 8 o'clock.
   Thirty minutes later she eats dinner.
   Draw the time on the clock when Ellen
   eats dinner.

What is your house or building number? Write it on a piece of paper. Then, write it in words. It is easy if you live at 15 Elm Street, but not so easy if you live at 15330 Martin Lane.

133

▶ A Sticky Situation

Having integrity means showing what you believe through your actions. Read the following situation. Below, write about what you would do.

Situation: You know that it is important to be honest. One day when you are playing at your best friend's house, she accidentally breaks her mom's cookie jar. She glues the pieces together and places it back on a table. Later in the day, her mom finds you two playing and questions both of you about the cookie jar. What would you do?

_____

_____

_____

_____

_____

_____

If your neighborhood has sidewalks and gutters, go "boating" after a storm. Drop a stick into the rushing water in the street. Chase your "boat" as it floats down the street. Does it disappear into the gutter? Make up a story about where it goes.

Count the money. Write each amount.

1.   _____ ¢

2.   _____ ¢

3.   _____ ¢

4. _____ ¢

5. _____ ¢

Some American Indians had an interesting way to name their children. They used names that told about an event in the life of the child. Give your friends new names. Your friend who plays soccer could be "Many Goals." Your sister who sings could be "Singing Bird."

▶ Cross out each incorrectly used or misspelled word in the journal entry. Write the correct word above it.

September 14, 2011

Yesterday, we learn about colors in art. We make a color wheel. We found

out that there is three basic colors. They am called primary colors. Red, yellow,

and blue are primary colors. Primary colors mix to make other colors. Red

and yellow makes orange. Yellow and blue make green. Blue and red make

purple. Orange, green, and purple is secondary colors.

If you live near a pond or lake or any other water, get an adult to help you scoop up some water in a plastic bottle. Cap the bottle. Place it on a counter for a few hours. How does it look different?

Circle the meaning of each underlined word.

1. She has on a <u>dark</u> purple dress.

   A. night   B. not light

2. We were <u>safe</u> on the rock.

   A. without danger   B. place to keep things

3. Fernando had to be home before <u>dark</u>.

   A. morning   B. night

4. I took a <u>trip</u> to the museum.

   A. a visit   B. to stumble

5. The <u>bank</u> closes at five o'clock.

   A. place where money is kept   B. a steep hill

Make your own ball-toss game. Ask an adult to cut three holes in the bottom of a box. Make one hole large, one medium, and one small. Tilt the box against a tree and grab some plastic balls. Ready, aim, toss!

137

► **Complete each sentence by writing an adjective from the word bank.**

yellow	fluffy	strong

1. The _____ school bus drove down the street.

2. A _____ wind blew through the trees.

3. The _____ dog followed me home.

_____

4. Write an adjective to describe you. _____

5. Write an adjective to describe ice cream. _____

6. Write an adjective to describe your school. _____

7. Write an adjective to describe a bug. _____

8. Write an adjective to describe the playground. _____

Cut out coupons from the newspaper or flyers your family gets in the mail. Sort them into categories based on what they are used to buy. Put each group of coupons in a separate envelope and label it with the category. Next time your family goes shopping, you can bring your coupon envelopes. How much money can you save?

Look at the parts of the bird. Then, write the words in alphabetical order.

1. _____

2. _____

3. _____

4. _____

5. _____

beak

eye

wing

tail

feet

Grocery bags make great safari jackets. Cut out holes for your neck and arms. Add a rope belt and some binoculars. Tape on paper pockets to hold your treasures. Grab a map and canteen, and start your adventure quest!

139

▶ **Count the groups of money in each problem. Draw an X on the group that is worth more.**

1.
 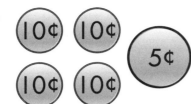

2.

3.

4.

Go on a bird-watching safari. Look for birds that live around your home. Try watching places birds like to go, like a bird feeder or bird nest. Draw a picture of each type of bird that you see. How many different birds can you find?

140

▶ **Adjectives** describe nouns. Some adjectives describe how things look or sound. Some adjectives describe how things feel or taste. Write the best adjective from the word bank to complete each sentence.

rainy	equal	low	tiny

1. I put an _____ amount of soup in my bowl and yours.

2. There is a _____ bug on the leaf.

3. Latoya stepped over the _____wall.

4. She saw a rainbow in the sky on the _____day.

Why do puddles disappear? After it rains, draw a line around a puddle on the sidewalk. For the next few days, draw a chalk line around the puddle at the same time each day. What is happening?

▶ **Read the passage. Then, answer the questions.**

Continents

Earth has seven continents: Africa, Antarctica, Asia, Australia, Europe, North America, and South America. These continents were once a large piece of land. The land split millions of years ago. Large pieces of land drifted apart. The oceans filled the spaces between the pieces of land. The continents we know today are the result. Each continent looks different and has different plants, animals, and weather. North America does not have tigers, but Asia does. Antarctica does not have a jungle, but South America does. The continents are similar in some ways. Some similarities may be because the continents were once one large piece of land.

1. What is the main idea of this passage?

   A. Earth is made of land and water.

   B. Earth has seven continents that were once one piece of land.

   C. Earth has many types of animals, plants, and weather.

2. What type of land can you find in South America? _____

3. Why might continents with an ocean between them have similarities?

   _____

   _____

A pizza box is a board game waiting to happen! Scrape off the cheese, then draw a game path on the inside of the bottom. In some spaces, write "Move ahead three" or "Lose a turn." Find some dice or a spinner, and some game pieces. After you play, shut the box to store the game.

► **Make one dollar in change five different ways.**

EXAMPLE:

quarters	2
dimes	4
nickels	2
pennies	0
total	$ 1.00

1. quarters _____

dimes _____

nickels _____

pennies _____

total $ _____

2. quarters _____

dimes _____

nickels _____

pennies _____

total $ _____

3. quarters _____

dimes _____

nickels _____

pennies _____

total $ _____

4. quarters _____

dimes _____

nickels _____

pennies _____

total $ _____

5. quarters _____

dimes _____

nickels _____

pennies _____

total $ _____

Instead of setting up a lemonade stand, try selling dog treats. Set up a table near a dog-walking route. Charge 5¢ a biscuit. Provide a big bowl of free water for thirsty customers.

▶ **Circle the adjectives in each sentence.**

EXAMPLE:

The (big)(red) wagon rolled down the hill.

1. Justin likes a soft pillow.

2. The hikers climbed a steep hill.

3. The door made a screechy noise.

4. The hot, wet sand felt good on our feet.

5. A breeze blew in the open window.

6. My sister skated on the slippery ice.

7. We lay on our backs in the soft, green grass.

8. The cold lemonade tasted good on such a warm day.

Use magazine letters to write a secret, nice note to a friend. Ask an adult for a magazine and some scissors. Cut out letters from the magazine. Glue them to a piece of paper to write your note. Mail your note, and do not forget your return address. It is a clue to the sender!

► **Read the words in each jar.**
Write the words in alphabetical order on the lines below the jar.

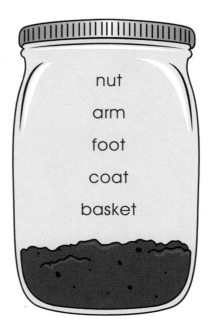

nut

arm

foot

coat

basket

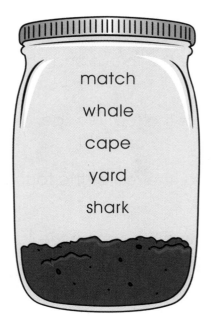

match

whale

cape

yard

shark

1. _____

2. _____

3. _____

4. _____

5. _____

6. _____

7. _____

8. _____

9. _____

10. _____

Do not wait for the sun in order to have a picnic.
Spread out a blanket inside. Use paper plates and
napkins. Pack a bottle of water. Can you make a
meal that has all the food groups?

▶ **Follow the directions.**

1. Color the toucan's beak three different colors.

2. Color the throat and chest orange.

3. Color the feet orange.

4. Color the rest of the toucan black.

5. Draw a branch for the toucan to sit on.

Are the ceiling fans in your house turning the right way? Stand under your fan and look up. If the fan is turning counterclockwise (the opposite way a clock's hands turn), then you should feel air blowing on you. That will cool you off in the summer. Fans should turn clockwise in the winter.

▶ Circle the object that costs more.

1.

 60¢    35¢

▶ Circle the coins you need to buy the guitar.

2.

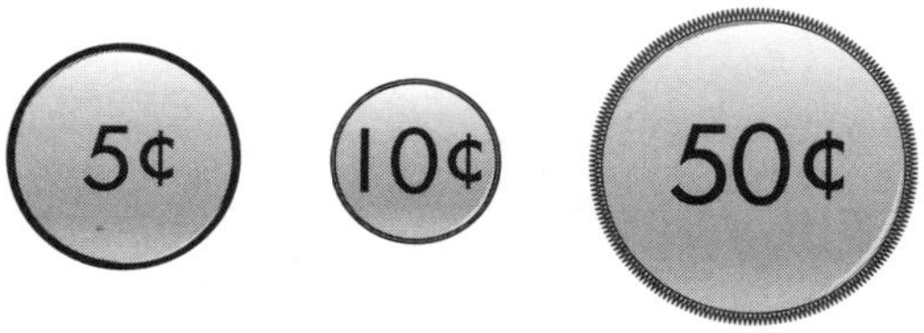

▶ Add the values of the coins in each group. Circle the correct amount.

3.

31¢   30¢   20¢

4.

15¢   20¢   11¢

 Start a collection of cool stuff. What is cool stuff? Whatever you like! You could collect rocks, coins, marbles, stamps, dolls, toy cars, or anything else that you enjoy. Store your collection in clear plastic boxes. Or, display it on a shelf in your room.

147

▶ **Write about something that you could reuse or recycle. How would you reuse or recycle it?**

_____

_____

_____

_____

_____

_____

_____

_____

_____

_____

If you have plastic eggs, drag them out for an ice hunt. Enclose an ice cube inside of each egg and hide the eggs in the yard. As your friends find the eggs, they should dump the ice into a wading pool. The last friend who dumps in some ice is the first one to jump into the wading pool! Brr!

▶ **Draw an X on the exact coins you need to buy each item.**

1. pack of gum

42¢

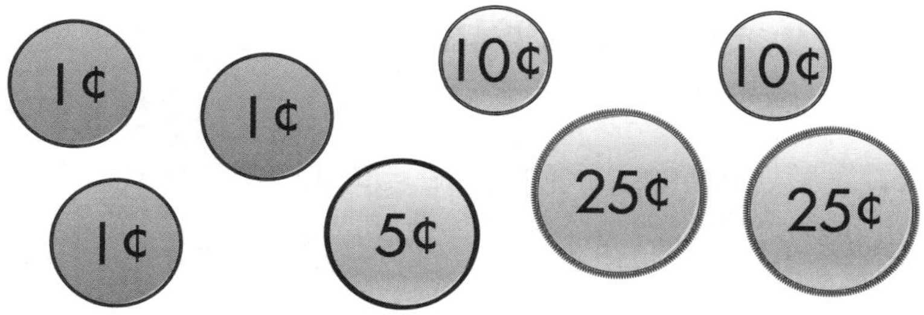

| 1¢ | 1¢ | 10¢ | 10¢ |
| 1¢ | 5¢ | 25¢ | 25¢ |

2. taffy

37¢

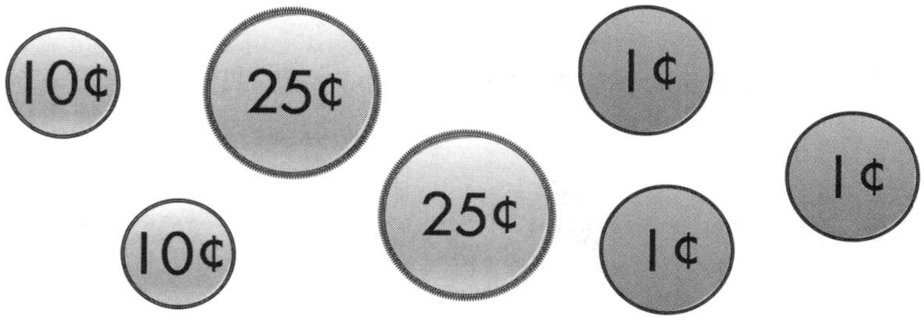

| 10¢ | 25¢ | 1¢ |
| 10¢ | 25¢ | 1¢ | 1¢ |

3. lemon drops

66¢

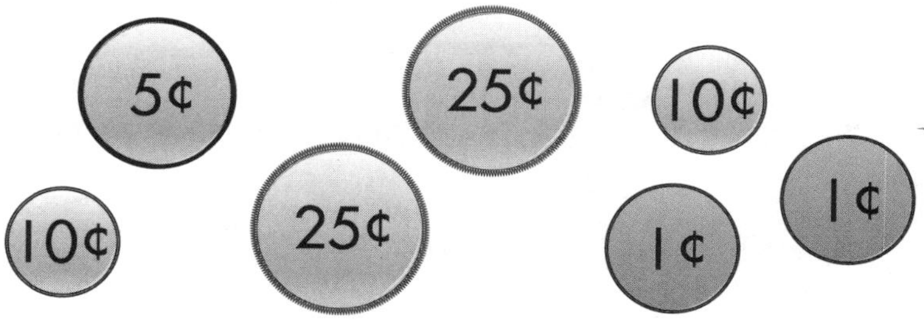

| 5¢ | 25¢ | 10¢ |
| 10¢ | 25¢ | 1¢ | 1¢ |

4. lollipop

73¢

1¢	5¢	10¢	1¢
1¢	1¢	25¢	
	10¢	10¢	25¢

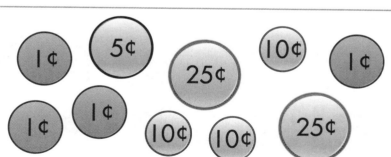

Flat flowers fade slowly. Gently spread out a flower between two small sheets of waxed paper. Stick it inside of a book. Pile on more books. Wait a couple of weeks, or until you want to read the book again, to see your preserved flower.

▶ **Circle the adjectives that describe each underlined noun.**

1. I have a blue and purple <u>coat</u>.

2. The little, green <u>snake</u> climbed the tree.

3. Tasha made a dress from colorful, soft <u>cloth</u>.

4. The dark, gray <u>cloud</u> is over my house.

5. I wore my new, brown <u>sandals</u> today.

6. He bought a white and red <u>ball</u>.

7. The furry, yellow <u>puppy</u> licked my nose.

Build a story from your favorite books. Pull out 10 books. In the first book, turn to page 10. Copy the third sentence. Repeat for the other nine books, then read the story. Did your story make you laugh?

▶ **Add or subtract to solve each problem.**

1.	28 + 18	**2.**	23 – 16	**3.**	46 – 27	**4.**	38 + 34

5.	77 – 38	**6.**	49 + 23	**7.**	58 + 35	**8.**	85 – 78

9.	48 – 29	**10.**	49 + 15	**11.**	96 – 37	**12.**	68 + 27

13.	47 – 39	**14.**	55 + 37	**15.**	71 – 24	**16.**	57 + 26

Make cleaning your room a breeze. Put away one kind of thing at a time. Start by putting away just your books, until no books are left. Next, put away just socks, or just dolls, or just action figures. The last thing you put away should be your favorite thing to play with.

► Read the story. Then, number the events in the order that they happened.

Snowed In

It snowed for three days. When it stopped, the snow was so deep that Ivan and Jacob could not open the cabin door. The men climbed through the upstairs window to get outside. They spent hours shoveling the snow away from the door. At last, they could open the door.

1. _____ The men climbed out the window.

2. _____ It snowed for three days.

3. _____ Ivan and Jacob opened the door.

4. _____ The men shoveled snow for hours.

Play this game at the grocery store or farmers' market. Search for a food that begins with each letter of the alphabet. Can you find a food to match each letter?

▶ Quick-Crawling Crab

Have you ever seen a crab crawling on the beach? If you try to move like those fast crustaceans, you can build your upper body, lower body, and core strength.

Sit on the floor. Place your hands behind you and feet in front of you flat on the ground. Use your arms and legs to lift your body off of the ground. Now, crab-walk backward a few yards. Then, crab-walk forward. It is hard to keep your weight off the ground for long!

Once you have mastered the crab-walk, you can make the activity more challenging. Use a stopwatch or timer to see how long you can crab-walk, or try to crab-walk faster. Practice the crab-walk throughout the summer, and you will feel your body become stronger.

Which way is the wind blowing? Pick up a few pieces of grass and toss them in the air, watching which way they move in the wind. You may have to do this a few times to be sure of the direction.

► **Find the length of each line segment in inches. Round each number to the nearest inch. Write the measurements in the boxes. Then, add the measurements.**

1.

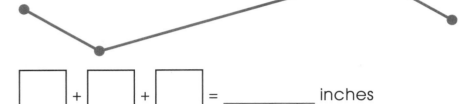

☐ + ☐ + ☐ = _____ inches

2.

☐ + ☐ + ☐ = _____ inches

3.

☐ + ☐ + ☐ = _____ inches

Serve it up in a game of volleyball. Use the hand you do not write with to toss the ball in the air about two feet higher than your head. Punch or slap the ball with your other hand. Aim it slightly up in the air so that it will clear the net.

► **Number the sentences in each group 1–4 to show the correct order.**

A.

_____ Brooke chased lightning bugs.

_____ The jar broke and the bugs flew away.

_____ She caught two lightning bugs.

_____ Brooke put the lightning bugs in a jar.

B. _____ Sharon came home from school.

_____ Sharon made a sandwich.

_____ Sharon ate a sandwich.

_____ Sharon went to the kitchen.

Fine-tune your library search. Think of a book you really enjoyed reading. Write the author's name on a piece of paper. Take the paper with you. At the library, look for a different book by the same author. Maybe you will enjoy it too.

► **Add the suffixes -*er* and -*est* to each word.**

EXAMPLE:

small   _____**smaller**_____   _____**smallest**_____

1. fast   _____   _____

2. tall   _____   _____

3. cold   _____   _____

4. light   _____   _____

5. warm   _____   _____

How do you find a river in a book? Not the word *river*, but a river between words. Open a chapter book and squint your eyes so that the print blurs and the white space between words stands out. Can you find a long, squiggly row of white space? This is called a river.

▶ **Measure in inches from dot to dot. Add the numbers to find each answer.**

1. _____ inches

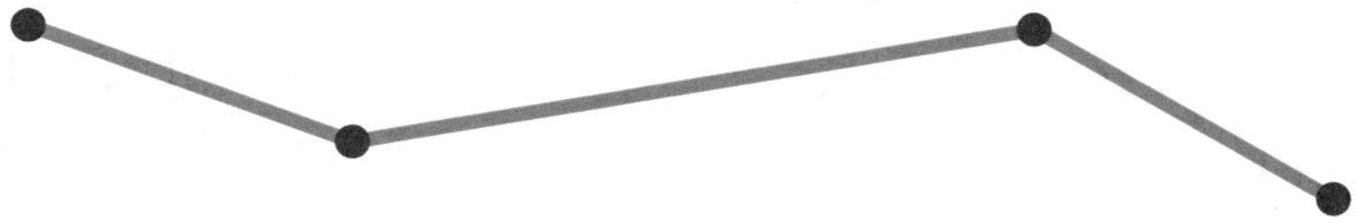

2. _____ inches

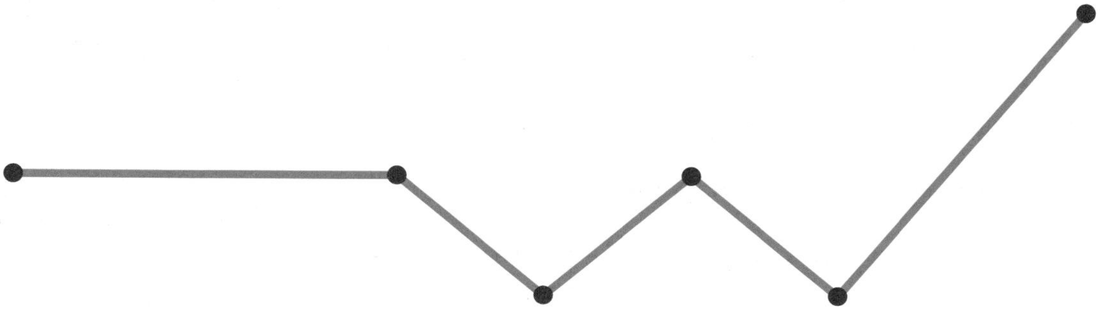

3. _____ inches

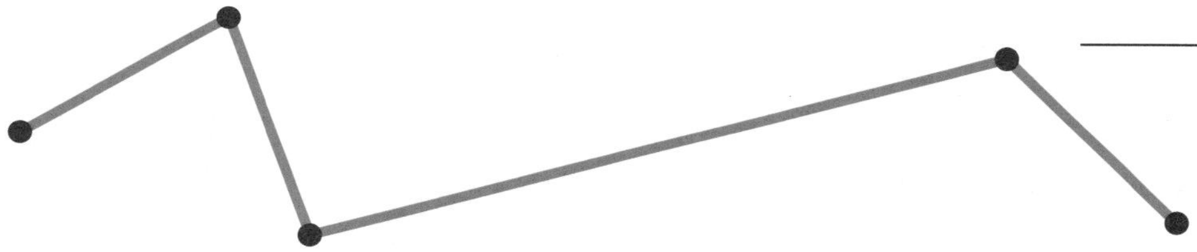

4. _____ inches

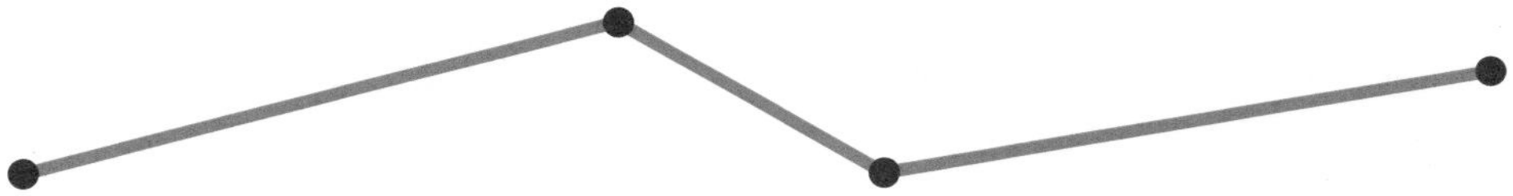

Cool off after your outdoor quests. Scoop ice cream or frozen yogurt in a blender. Add frozen, chopped fruit and three drops of vanilla. Toss in a couple of ice cubes. Ask an adult to blend the drink, then pour it into a glass and drink it with a straw. Refreshing!

▶ **Read the passage. Then, answer the questions.**

Sleep

Are you ever sleepy in the middle of the day? Children need about 8 to 11 hours of sleep each night. During sleep, your body rests and gets ready for another day. It is important to be rested for school every morning. If you are tired, you might have trouble paying attention to your teacher. If you have a hard time falling asleep, try reading a book instead of watching TV before bedtime. Go to bed at the same time every night. Play soft music to help you get sleepy. Soon, you will be dreaming!

1. What is the main idea of this passage?

   A. Getting enough sleep is important.

   B. Reading a book can help you go to sleep.

   C. You should dream every night.

2. How much sleep do children need? _____

3. What might happen at school if you are tired? _____

   _____

4. What can you do instead of watching TV at bedtime? _____

   _____

Make your own calendar—sort of. Ask an adult for a current calendar that is not being used. Draw or paint a picture that shows what you like about each month. Glue your pictures over the calendar pictures.

▶ Measure the length of each object in centimeters.

1.  _____ cm

2.  _____ cm

3.  _____ cm

4.  _____ cm

5.  _____ cm

6.  _____ cm

Borrow a trick from an old saying to test what kind of mood your friends are in. Fill a glass halfway with milk. Ask your friends if the glass is half empty or half full. Are the friends who see the glass as half full in a better mood than the friends who see it as half empty?

► **Write an adjective to complete each sentence.**

1. Gabriel showed me the _____ picture.

2. The _____ puppy is chasing his tail.

3. That _____ bird flies south for the winter.

4. Stephen carried the _____ suitcase.

5. That book with the _____ cover is mine.

6. The _____ lizard is sitting on a rock.

7. I will wear the _____ shirt tomorrrow.

Go on a quest for some serious giggles by playing Belly Laugh! Have your friend lie down, then gently place your head on your friend's belly. Tell your friend to laugh. Can either of you stop laughing?

▶ **Circle the letter next to the main idea of each paragraph.**

1. Sometimes I have strange dreams. Once, I dreamed I was floating inside a spaceship. When I woke up, I thought I was still floating. I reminded myself that it was just a dream. When I told my mom about it, she said that she sometimes has strange dreams too.

   A. I dreamed I was floating in space.

   B. My mom had the same dream I did.

   C. Sometimes we have strange dreams.

2. I like to read. In the summer, I go to the library twice a week. I check out books about lemurs and airplanes. I also like to read about rain forests. The librarian helps me find books I will like.

   A. I read books about race cars in the summer.

   B. I find books to read at the library.

   C. Librarians are friendly and helpful.

Bring the great outdoors inside. Ask an adult for two very large pieces of paper. On one paper, paint an outdoor scene. On the other, paint a matching sky. Get an adult's help to tape the papers above your bed and on your wall.

► **Choose the best adjective from the word bank to complete each sentence.**

funny	red	hard	oak	six	furry

1. His kite got caught in that _____ tree.

2. I can't believe you ate _____ hot dogs!

3. At the circus, we laughed at the _____ clowns.

4. Jackie got a _____ bike for Christmas.

5. My pillow is very _____ and lumpy.

6. The rabbits all had soft and _____ ears.

Looking for a way to fool your brain? Put a piece of paper on a table and tilt a mirror over the paper. Look into the mirror and try to write your name. Can you do it?

► **Read each word. Change the underlined letter or letters to make a new word.**

EXAMPLE:

<u>pr</u>ess _____mess_____

1. <u>t</u>ake _____

2. <u>w</u>ell _____

3. th<u>o</u>se _____

4. <u>d</u>ove _____

5. <u>sh</u>ip _____

6. <u>t</u>rue _____

7. b<u>u</u>d _____

8. <u>f</u>ast _____

9. <u>r</u>ide _____

10. <u>l</u>ike _____

11. <u>m</u>ist _____

You can control water! Take a glass filled with water outside. Cover the glass with an index card, making sure the edges are completely covered. Hold the card against the glass, and turn it over. Slowly take your hand off the card. Wow, how did you do that?

▶ One meter is 100 centimeters. Circle your estimate for each question.

EXAMPLE:

A dictionary is

A. taller than one meter.

B. shorter than one meter. *(circled)*

1. A house is

A. taller than one meter.

B. shorter than one meter.

2. A baby is

A. longer than one meter.

B. shorter than one meter.

3. Your front door is

A. taller than one meter.

B. shorter than one meter.

4. A pencil is

A. longer than one meter.

B. shorter than one meter.

5. A paper clip is

A. longer than one meter.

B. shorter than one meter.

Discover the secret lives of people around you. As someone walks by, imagine a story about him. Where is he going? What does he do? Maybe he trains circus dogs. Maybe he raises poodles and Saint Bernards. Try to imagine a story from start to finish.

▶ **Write the two words that make each contraction.**

EXAMPLE:

hasn't _____ **has not** _____

1. we'd _____

2. you'll _____

3. she's _____

4. we've _____

5. I'll _____

6. you're _____

7. don't _____

8. isn't _____

9. can't _____

10. I'm _____

11. could've _____

12. wouldn't _____

13. won't _____

Go on a quest for odd talent. Ask your friends and family what odd talents they have. Maybe your brother can touch his nose with his tongue. Can your dad raise just one eyebrow? Maybe your best friend can sing the alphabet backwards. Convince your friends to have an odd talent show.

▶ **Measure in centimeters from dot to dot. Add the numbers to find each answer.**

1.

_____ cm

2.

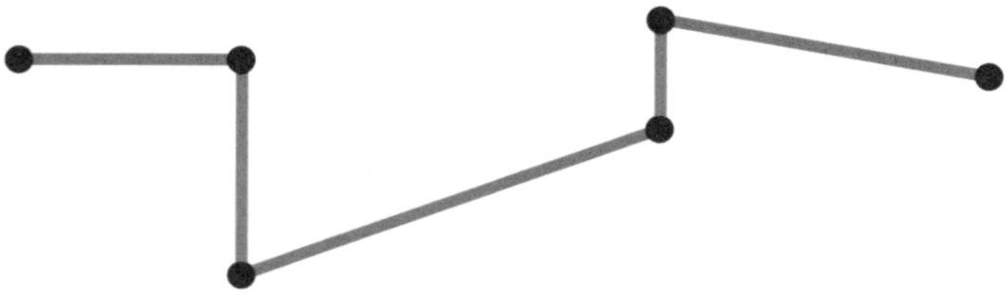

_____ cm

3.

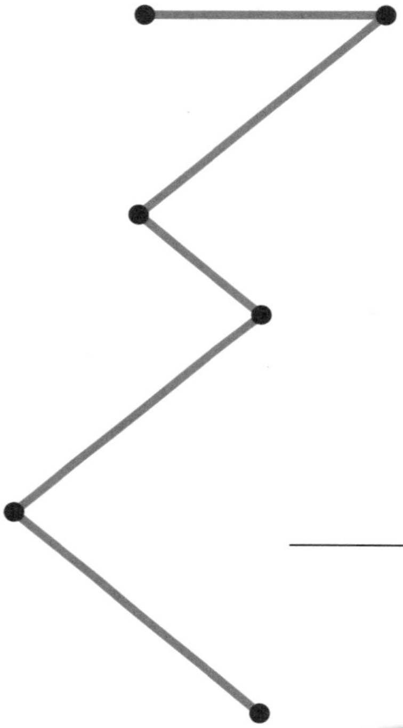

_____ cm

4.

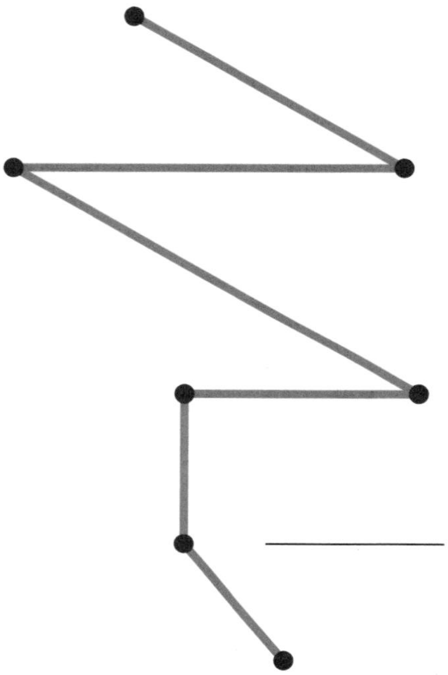

_____ cm

It is no fun to be sick. Hunt for some treats that will keep you busy next time you are sick. In a box, put some new crayons and paper. Add a favorite book or a new one, or a puzzle book. Put in some extra-comfy pajamas. Add any other stuff that will make you feel better. Put the box under your bed for your next sick day.

▶ **Use the table of contents to answer the questions.**

Table of Contents

1. On which page should you begin reading about where ants live?

_____

2. Which chapter would tell about the different kinds of ants?

_____

3. On which page would you look to find the index?

_____

4. What is the title of the first chapter?

_____

All you need to be a super hero or heroine is a cape. Ask an adult to let you cut a hole in one end of an old towel, and cut off the top corners. Stick your head through the hole and save the world!

▶ **The main idea of a story is what the story is all about. Read each story. Underline the phrase that tells the main idea of the story.**

1. Lisa's dog, Fletcher, knows quite a lot of tricks. They're all very nice tricks, but they are unusual. Fletcher can turn the television on by pushing the button with his nose. He turns on the garden hose with his paw when he wants a drink. Fletcher has even learned to open the mailbox. Lisa thinks that bringing in the mail is Fletcher's best trick.

A. Fletcher's unusual tricks

B. Lisa's dog

C. Fletcher gets a drink

2. Ryan stood looking in the bakery window for a long time. He just could not make up his mind which cake he wanted. The one with the chocolate icing looked good. Ryan also saw one that had nuts all over the top. He was ready to get that one when another cake caught his eye. There in front of him was a cake with white icing. All over the top were piled the biggest strawberries Ryan had ever seen. How would he decide?

A. The strawberry cake

B. Ryan's difficult decision

C. The bakery

Here is a silly trick. Show your friends a black magic marker. Tell them you have an amazing rainbow marker that will write any color you tell it to. Ask a friend what color she wants you to write. When she says, "purple," write the word *purple* on a piece of paper. Ha ha!

► **Draw an X over each misspelled word. Write each word correctly.**

1. Marcus has a new electrik car. _____

2. Bonnie takes the fast trane to work. _____

3. Let's keap together when we go. _____

4. My dad drives a large dump truk. _____

5. Let's plae baseball. _____

6. The snowflakes fel very quickly. _____

7. I put on my soks. _____

Ask a group of friends to play a game of Guess What I Ate? Ask each friend to tell a story about something yucky she ate. It can be true or pretend. After each friend takes a turn, guess whether or not the story is true.

▶ **Circle the object in each row that holds the most.**

1.

2.

3.

 You can see a rainbow up close. Fill a shallow glass pan with water. Place it in a patch of sunlight, and move it around until you see a rainbow on the wall. Look at it closely. Can you see all of the colors in the rainbow?

▶ Write the two words that make each contraction.

1. she's _____

2. I'd _____

3. aren't _____

4. haven't _____

5. I've _____

6. shouldn't _____

7. it's _____

8. we're _____

9. she'll _____

10. isn't _____

11. we'll _____

12. you'll _____

13. he's _____

14. we've _____

15. you've _____

16. they'll _____

Make jewelry while you weed the lawn. Pick dandelions with long, thick stems. Gently tie one stem around another. Tie the knot just under the flower, then tie that flower's stem under a new flower. Keep tying until the necklace is longer than you want. Tie the last stem to the first flower to finish.

► **Read the passage. Then, answer the questions.**

Changing with the Seasons

We change the types of clothes we wear with the seasons to protect us from the weather. Animals do the same when the seasons change.

For example, the arctic fox has a thick, white fur coat in the winter. A white coat is not easy to see in the snow. This helps the fox hide. When spring comes, the fox's fur changes to brown or gray. It becomes the color of the ground.

The ptarmigan bird, or snow chicken, has white feathers in the winter. It, too, is hard to see in the snow. In the spring, the bird **molts**. This means that it sheds all of its feathers. The bird grows new feathers that are gray or brown and speckled. When the bird is very still, it looks like a rock.

1. What is the passage mostly about?

   A. how people change with the seasons

   B. how seasons change

   C. how animals change with the seasons

2. What happens to the ptarmigan bird in the spring?

   A. It molts.   B. It flies south.

   C. Its feathers turn red.   D. It hides near rocks.

3. What does **molt** mean in the story?

   A. to change colors   B. to shed feathers

   C. to hide from an enemy   D. to run quickly

Make a rock wall for your action figures or dolls to climb. Find a handful of small rocks. Ask an adult to use superglue to attach the rocks to a wooden board or a piece of heavy cardboard. Lean the rock wall against a tree. Let your toys start climbing!

► **Write the temperature on the first line. Then, write if it is warm or cold.**

1.

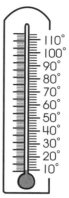

_____ °F

_____

2.

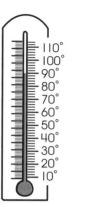

_____ °F

_____

3.

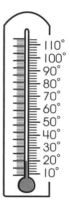

_____ °F

_____

4.

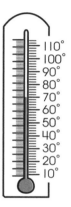

_____ °F

_____

If your family uses napkins or coasters, they probably stick to the bottom of your glasses. Try to think of a way to make the coasters stay on the table. Need a hint? All you need is a saltshaker.

▶ **Circle and write the correct contraction to complete each sentence.**

EXAMPLE:

_____**They've**_____ never played tennis.

They're   They'll   (They've)

1. _____ have a really fun time.

We're   We'll   We've

2. _____ work as hard as I can.

I'm   I've   I'll

3. _____ got to do it right the first time.

We've   We'll   We're

4. _____ going to see a movie tonight.

We'll   We're   We've

Write an *H* on one side of a craft stick and a *T* on the other. Tell your friends that you are going to flip the stick like a coin. Ask whether they think it will land on *H* or *T*. After they choose, say that you think it will land on its side. No way! Bend the craft stick in half without breaking it, then toss it in the air and watch it land on its side.

▶ **Read the story about Max and Julia. Write _M_ beside the phrases that describe Max, and _J_ beside the phrases that describe Julia. Write _B_ if the phrase describes both children.**

Max and Julia

Max and Julia are twins. They have brown eyes and black hair. They are eight years old and go to school. Julia likes math, and Max likes to read. They both like to play outside. Julia likes to play basketball. Max likes to run and play tag. Julia likes to ride her bike while Max walks their dog, Rover.

1. _____ has brown eyes

2. _____ likes to run

3. _____ is a twin

4. _____ likes to play basketball

5. _____ likes to read

6. _____ likes math

7. _____ is eight

8. _____ has a pet

9. _____ likes to ride bikes

10. _____ has black hair

You need a helper for this trick. After drinking a drink through a straw, wrap the ends of the straw around your index fingers. Leave about an inch between them. Ask your friend to flick the straw between your fingers. Pop! Hope you finished that drink! What happens to the straw?

▶ **Write the letter of the correct definition next to each vocabulary word.**

1. _____ desert   A. a tall piece of land

2. _____ mountain   B. a flowing body of water

3. _____ valley   C. a body of water surrounded by land

4. _____ ocean   D. low land between mountains or hills

5. _____ lake   E. a place that is very dry

6. _____ river   F. a body of water that surrounds
                                  continents

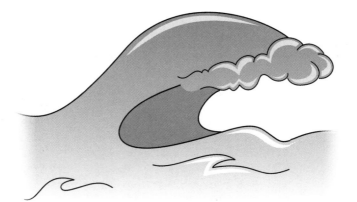

Ask an adult if you can listen to his half of a phone conversation. Jot down what he says for five minutes. Fill in a pretend conversation between the lines. Make it as silly as you can. Read it out loud when the adult is off the phone.

▶ **This baby eagle needs help. Read the story to learn more about it.**

A High Flyer

Deke is a baby bald eagle who is learning to fly. It has been a real hardship for Deke. He has been practicing for days. He just does not seem to be improving.

Getting up in the air was easy. Flying over the plains was no problem. But Deke has trouble flying around things. He does not do well when he attempts to land on a certain spot, either. It is hard for Deke to face his friends. Perhaps he should sign up for flying lessons to better his flying skills.

▶ **Write the letter of the best answer on each line.**

_____ **1.** The word **hardship** means:

A. something that is not easy   B. a boat   C. a broken wing   D. stony

_____ **2.** The word **improving** means:

A. getting better   B. feeling sad   C. feeling sore   D. getting lost

_____ **3.** A word in the story that means the **opposite of hairy** is:

A. problem   B. practicing   C. around   D. bald

_____ **4.** In the story, the word **He** stands for:

A. Deke's friend   B. Deke   C. Deke's dad   D. the teacher

Use art as inspiration for a story. Look around your house, an office, or a museum. Find a painting or picture you really like. Imagine that one of the people in the picture is on a secret quest. Write a tale about the quest. Read it to your family in front of the picture.

▶ **Names of days of the week begin with capital letters. Answer each question with the correct names of the days.**

1. Write the names of the three days that have exactly six letters. _____

_____

2. Which day comes after Friday? _____

3. Which two days have names with exactly eight letters? _____

_____

4. _____ has exactly seven letters, and _____ has nine.

 Be adventurous at the grocery store. On your next trip, pick out three foods you have never eaten before. Ask an adult for help. Try the new foods over the next few meals. Did you find any new favorites?

► Read the sentences. Follow the directions to draw the picture.

1. Draw blue water across the space.

2. Draw a green boat on the water.

3. Draw three people in the boat.

4. Draw five seagulls in the sky.

5. Draw a fishing pole at the back of the boat.

6. Draw two large fish in the water.

Give your friend her marching orders. Make up a rhyming song to sing. It should have a strong beat to keep you in step. Sing it loudly and clearly as you march around together.

▶ **To abbreviate a word means to shorten it. Draw a line to match each word to its abbreviation.**

1. December   Dr.

     Doctor   oz.

     Thursday   Dec.

     ounce   Jan.

     January   Thurs.

2. Mister   Rd.

     October   ft.

     foot   Mr.

     Avenue   Ave.

     Road   Oct.

3. yard   Jr.

     March   Wed.

     Junior   yd.

     inch   in.

     Wednesday   Mar.

4. Saturday   Sr.

     Senior   St.

     Monday   Mon.

     Fahrenheit   F

     Street   Sat.

Photos help make a newspaper story come alive. Pretend to be a photographer for a paper. Go on a quest to snap a great shot. Ask an adult to cut out some headlines for you. Glue each headline to a piece of drawing paper. Draw the picture you "took" below it.

► **Write each number in standard form on the line.**

A number is usually written using digits in the appropriate place value spots. This is called standard form.

EXAMPLES: five thousand, two hundred, fifty-one = **5,251**
twenty-two thousand, thirty-three = **22,033**

1. six hundred thirty-four = _____

2. eight thousand, two hundred fifty-one = _____

3. nine thousand, three hundred twenty-two = _____

4. twenty-seven thousand, eight hundred = _____

5. seventy thousand, one hundred two = _____

6. eighty-three thousand, three hundred eleven = _____

7. fourteen thousand, seven hundred sixty = _____

Have a little brother or sister to entertain? Here is a great way to keep a sibling busy and happy. Grab a bed sheet. Ask your sibling to hold one side of it while you hold the other, then flap it up in the air together. Dive under the sheet together before it hits the ground.

▶ **Write the words from the word bank in alphabetical order.**

her	are	third
card	bud	dark
turn	more	part
word	bird	first

1. _____

2. _____

3. _____

4. _____

5. _____

6. _____

7. _____

8. _____

9. _____

10. _____

11. _____

12. _____

If you have a big box of crayons, dump them out. Put all of the shades of green together, all of the reds together, and so on. Which color is most popular? Why are there so many of some colors? Are there some that stand alone?

► **Many doors lead to interesting places and things. Think of a door that could lead you to an interesting place. Describe the door and what is behind it. In the box below, draw a picture of your door.**

_____

_____

_____

_____

_____

Play tricks on your own eyes. Hold the end of a pencil between your thumb and index finger. Hold the pencil horizontally in front of your face. "Bounce" the pencil up and down in front of your face. Does the pencil still look straight?

▶ **Write the name of each shape.**

1.

_____

2.

_____

3.

_____

4.

_____

5.

_____

6.

_____

7.

_____

8.

_____

9.

_____

 Make your own safari pith helmet by mixing flour, water, and glue into a paste. Blow up a balloon. Cover the top half with strips of newspaper dipped in the paste. When it dries, pop the balloon. Glue a wide strip of paper bag around the bottom for the brim. Now you are ready for jungle heat and desert sun!

▶ **Write *yes* if the sentence is complete. Write *no* if it is not complete.**

EXAMPLE:

Inside a large.   no

1. Someone is walking on the sidewalk.   _____

2. I went to a movie last night.   _____

3. Played in the park by.   _____

4. What is the?   _____

5. Under the swing in front of the house.   _____

6. Every Sunday afternoon.   _____

7. Did you enjoy reading that book?   _____

 Does your cat need to go on a diet? Your cat may not sit on a scale, but you can still weigh her. Hold your cat, step on the scale, and then write down the weight. As your cat runs away, weigh just yourself. Subtract this weight from the first one. How much does your cat weigh?

► **Read the poem. Then, answer the questions.**

Two

Two living things, blowing in the wind.
One stands straight, the other bends.

One is a strong tree growing tall.
The other is grass ever so small.

Both are Mother Nature's gifts.
The tree you can climb. On the grass, you can sit.

Green is their color, brought on by the spring.
Grass or trees, they both make me sing!

1. What two things is the poem comparing?
   A. the grass and a tree
   B. a tree and a flower
   C. the wind and the rain

2. Read each description. Decide if the words describe the grass, a tree, or both. Write an X in each correct column.

Alike or Different	Grass	Tree
living thing		
stands straight in the wind		
bends in the wind		
tall		
small		

When you go on a quest, carry a first-aid kit. Find a plastic box with a lid. Add bandages, antibacterial ointment, and wipes for cuts. Add tweezers, gauze, a cold compress, and a big bandage. Now you are ready for some bumps in the road.

► **Can you dunk a glass with a paper towel inside it into an aquarium filled with water and have the paper towel stay dry?**

Materials:
- large, clear container or aquarium
- drinking glass (any size)
- dry paper towel
- water

Procedure:

Have an adult help you fill the aquarium with water.

Gently stuff the paper towel into the bottom of the glass. Turn the glass upside down, but make sure that the paper towel does not fall out.

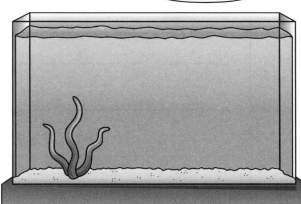

Keep the glass upside down. Slowly lower it straight down into the container of water until the paper towel and glass are both completely underwater. (Note: the experiment will not work if you tilt the glass at all.) Remove the glass from the water. Is the paper towel wet or dry?

What's This All About?

This experiment shows that air takes up space. As you lower the glass into the container of water, the air inside the glass displaces, or pushes away, the water in the container. Because the water is displaced, the paper towel stays dry.

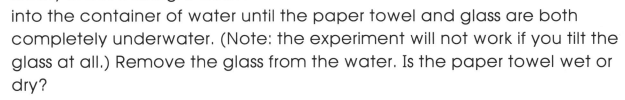

Write a jingle (a song) for your favorite healthy snack food. Ask a few friends to sing it with you. If you can, ask an adult to tape the commercial. Do you think your jingle would sell more healthy foods?

► **Practice writing a letter on this page.**
Then, write a letter on real stationery and send it to someone special.

There are five parts to a friendly letter:
the **date**, **greeting**, **body**, **closing**, and **signature**.

_____
(date)

_____
(greeting)

_____
(body of letter)

_____

_____

_____

_____

_____

_____,
(closing)

_____
(signature)

Here is a great quest for your brain. Teach it to multitask. First, try to rub your stomach and pat your head at the same time. Next, add walking to this task. After that, twirl one of your feet in the air, then try to twirl your finger in the opposite direction. Can you do it? Why do you think this is difficult?

▶ **Which would drop faster if it fell from a two-story building: a penny or a sheet of paper? Which would hit the ground first? How does air affect falling objects?**

Materials:
- several sheets of paper
- penny
- a few small, unbreakable objects

Procedure:

Hold the penny and the sheet of paper in front of you and higher than your head. Let them both fall at the same time. Repeat this activity two more times.

Now, crumple the paper into a tight ball. Hold the paper and the penny in front of you and higher than your head. Let them both fall at the same time. Repeat this activity two more times.

Repeat the experiment with two sheets of paper that are crumpled, one loosely and one tightly. Then, try different coins and other objects. Which object falls the fastest?

What's This All About?

Even though we cannot see air, it has force. By crumpling the paper, you reduced the amount of force the air was able to put on the paper. We call this force *friction*.

Sometimes it is good to have a lot of air friction. For example, a person using a parachute would want friction. The friction created by the parachute would slow her fall to Earth. Sometimes it is good to have less air friction, such as a pilot trying to go fast in an airplane.

Write some words in red marker. Make sure the letters are pretty thick and colored in. Next, color the rest of the page with medium blue marker. Shake the paper in front of you. Can you make the words jump off the page?

© Rainbow Bridge Publishing

▶ A **grid** (set of lines on a map) and **coordinates** (the letters and numbers beside the grid) help you locate places on a map. To find the mall on the map, look at section B,2. Use the map grid and map key to fill in the blanks with the coordinates for each place.

Map Key

✈ = airport

🖊 = school

⛳ = golf course

🌲 = park

🛍 = mall

✚ = hospital

🐟 = lake

🏊 = swimming pool

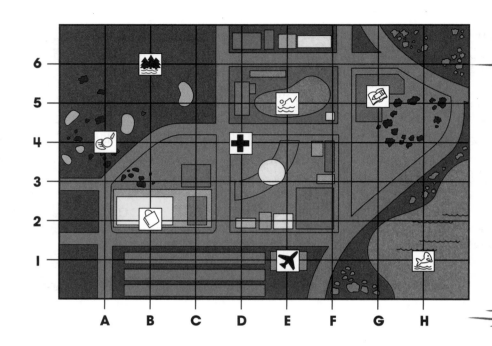

EXAMPLE:

mall _____**B, 2**_____

1. lake _____

2. school _____

3. park _____

4. airport _____

5. hospital _____

6. golf course _____

7. swimming pool _____

Write messages on sticky notes such as, "Look on the dryer," and "Check the back door." Leave the notes all over the house in the correct order. Place a little treat next to the last one. Start a sibling or a friend at the first message. Did he like the treasure hunt?

► **Read the paragraph below. Then, answer the questions using complete sentences.**

Dinosaurs

Millions of years ago, dinosaurs lived on Earth. The word "dinosaur" means "terrible lizard." Some dinosaurs were 30 times bigger than an elephant. Many dinosaurs ate plants, but some ate meat. Dinosaurs became extinct, or died out, a long time ago.

1. What does the word "dinosaur" mean?

   _____

2. When did dinosaurs live on Earth?

   _____

3. Did all dinosaurs eat plants?

   _____

4. How big were some dinosaurs?

   _____

Eye color and dimples are traits that you get from your parents. Dominant traits are more common. Recessive ones are less common. Who do you know with recessive traits such as attached earlobes, blue eyes, or being able to fold the tongue from front to back? Who has dominant traits such as dimples, rolling the tongue, or brown eyes?

▶ **Your favorite baseball team is in the championship game. Follow the steps to find out where your friends are sitting at the game**

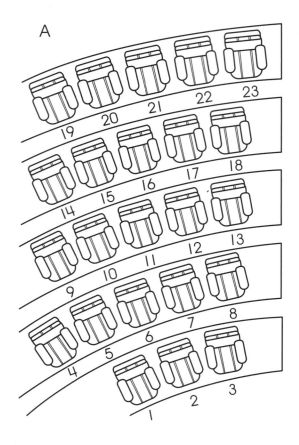

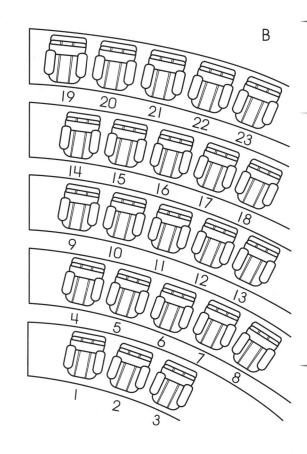

1. Greg is sitting in seat A, 11. Draw a red circle around Greg's seat.

2. Shauna is sitting in seat B, 9. Draw a blue square around Shauna's seat.

3. Craig is sitting in seat B, 5. Draw a green triangle around Craig's seat.

4. Phillip is sitting in seat A, 2. Color Phillip's seat orange.

5. Beth is sitting in seat A, 6. Color Beth's seat purple.

Is a black marker really black? Color a patch of paper towel with a washable black marker. Drop some water on the towel near the marker. What colors do you see?

▶ Take It Outside!

Go outside with an adult. Take a notebook, a pencil, and a ruler that measures inches and centimeters. Find objects. Measure their lengths. Record each object's length in inches and centimeters. Compare the measurements. Which objects are the shortest, and which are the longest?

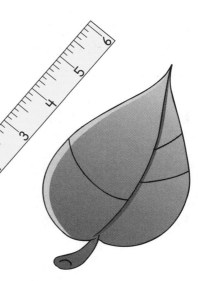

Play an outdoor observation game with a friend or family member. Find an object that is a three-dimensional geometric shape (sphere, cube, cylinder, cone, prism, or pyramid). Describe the shape to your friend. For example, to describe a beach ball, you would say, "I see a sphere." Take turns describing and identifying shapes.

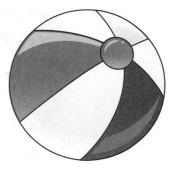

Help your friends "brace themselves" with friendship bracelets. Find some twine and beads. Cut three pieces of twine about 12" long and tie them together at one end. Close the knot in a book to hold it in place. Braid the twine and add a bead here and there. Tie the bottom to the other end, and you have made a bracelet!

▶ A **continent** is the largest landmass on Earth. There are seven continents in the world. List the seven continents by unscrambling each name. Then, look at the map. Write the letter of each continent next to its name.

1. _____ ACIFRA _____

2. _____ THORN MICAERA _____

3. _____ EPRUEO _____

4. _____ HOUTS RECIMAA _____

5. _____ SAAI _____

6. _____ CTARNATCAI _____

7. _____ STRLAIAUA _____

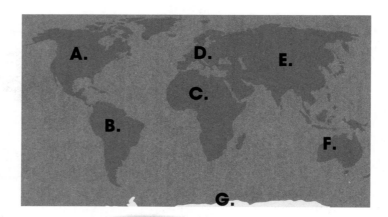

Sing with the doves. Put your thumbs side by side. Fold the fingers of one hand between your thumb and index finger. Wrap the fingers of your other hand around the back. Press your hands together. Blow on your thumb knuckles. Practice until you hear a hollow, whistling noise, then go call the doves. Do they answer?

▶ **Circle the sentence in each pair that makes sense.**

1. The ice is in the glass.   The glass is in the ice.

2. Put the porch on the plant.   Put the plant on the porch.

3. The desk is on the lamp.   The lamp is on the desk.

4. Please answer the phone.   Answer phone the please.

5. I will dog the walk.   I will walk the dog.

6. Lawn is good for the rain.   Rain is good for the lawn.

7. Did you see my keys?   Did my keys see you?

8. The piano plays Hugo.   Hugo plays the piano.

Get your pet hula-hoop to come when you call it. Grab a hoop. As you toss it away, snap your hand up as you release it so that the hoop spins back toward you. The hoop should bounce away and then change directions and come back. Be sure to call it as it starts rolling back.

▶ Take It Outside!

Go outside with an adult. Take a pencil and this page. List some actions that have already happened. Examples include a house that has been built (built), a child who passed by (walked), a man getting out of a car (drove). When you are finished, look at the past-tense verbs on your list. Write a sentence with each verb.

_____

_____

_____

_____

_____

_____

_____

These flips will not be a flop. Gather some beads, sequins, ribbons, and glue. Glue the items to the tops of the thongs of inexpensive flip-flops (not between your toes). Does anyone notice your decorated flip-flops?

► **Circle the shape in each row that represents the bottom face of the solid figure.**

1.

2.

3.

4.

Bored? Play Top This with your friends. Pick a category, such as songs on the radio, or names that start with *R*, or kinds of big cats. Take turns naming things that fit the category. As players cannot think of things that fit the category, they are out. The last player standing wins that round.

197

► **Read the stories. Circle what happens next.**

I. Jeff put his arms around the box. He could not lift it. He would need some help. The box was too heavy for him.

Jeff will_____ .

A. run outside and play

B. ask his dad for help

C. sit on the box

D. send the box to his friend

2. The children were playing outside. It started to get dark. They saw a flash of light and heard a loud sound. The wind began to blow.

"Let's go," shouted Hunter. "It's _____ ."

A. time to eat

B. going to blow us away

C. going to rain soon

D. time for bed

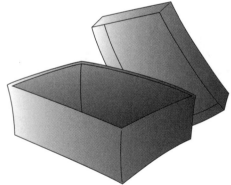

Count down to a favorite holiday. Find a calendar. Use it to help you count the number of days until that day. Write the number on today's date. Subtract one each day. Write the new number on that day's date. 3-2-1—celebrate!

► **Write each word from the word bank under the correct heading.**

ball	beans	blocks	bread	cheese	corn
doll	fox	horse	kite	monkey	tiger

Animals   **Toys**   **Food**

_____   _____   _____

_____   _____   _____

_____   _____   _____

_____   _____   _____

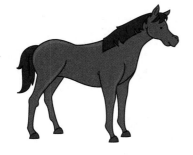

Open a restaurant *al fresco* (outside). Make some easy food. Try cheese and crackers, grapes, and lemonade. Write a menu. Set a table outside. Then, make the food, and invite some diners over.

▶ **Look at each solid figure. Each side is called a face. Write the number of faces for each solid.**

1. cube

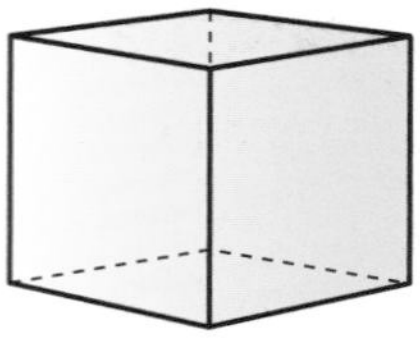

_____ ☐ faces

2. triangular prism

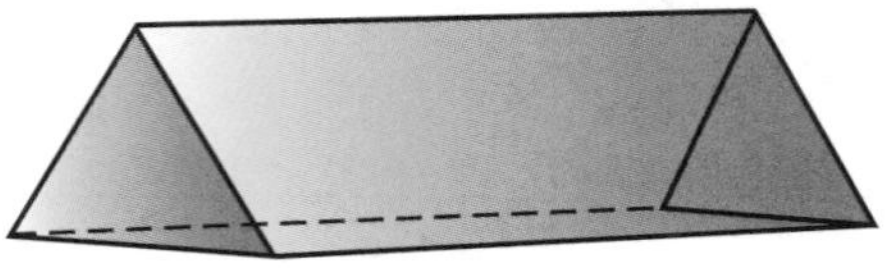

_____ △ faces   _____ ▭ faces

3. pyramid

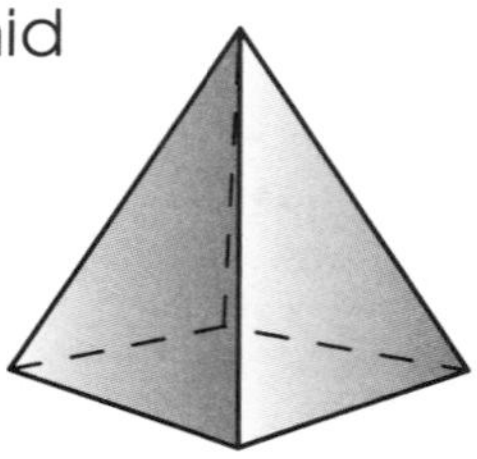

_____ ☐ faces   _____ △ faces

4. rectangular prism

_____ ☐ faces   _____ ▭ faces

You do not need a tennis court to play Big, Fat Tennis. Grab two rackets or even two plastic baseball bats. Find a big, fat plastic ball. Stand in an open area and hit the ball back and forth with a friend.

▶ A **declarative sentence** makes a statement. Write *D* for each declarative sentence. Write *ND* for each sentence that is not declarative.

1. _____ Carrots are good for you.

2. _____ Do you like to draw?

3. _____ My sister plays soccer.

4. _____ They went for a walk.

5. _____ How old are you?

6. _____ You could swim.

7. _____ What do you like to do?

8. _____ Have you tried karate?

9. _____ Erin washed her dishes.

10. _____ Apples are my favorite fruit.

Try this library scavenger hunt. Can you find an author whose name starts with *T*? How about a book about a dog, or a book with a rainbow on the cover? Can you find a book about a holiday? Jot down a few more ideas, then start searching!

▶ **Subtract to solve each problem. Remember to regroup. Use the code to solve the riddle.**

What did dinosaurs have that no other animal has ever had?

46	25	64	37	47	19	49	28	58	17
D	B	N	A	R	U	S	Y	O	I

1.

53 − 28	71 − 34	84 − 59	46 − 18

2.

63 − 17	75 − 58	92 − 28	84 − 26	63 − 14	96 − 59	37 − 18	66 − 19	65 − 16

Here is a meal you can make inside or outside. Push the soft part of a piece of bread into the cup of a muffin tin. Crack an egg on top. Add shredded cheese. Ask an adult to help you bake it in a 350° oven (or over a campfire) for about ten minutes, or until the cheese melts and the egg is firm. Yum!

▶ **Write the words in each sentence in alphabetical order. Begin each sentence with a capital letter. The first one has been done for you.**

EXAMPLE:

talk did she with you?_____ _Did she talk with you?_____

1. I notebook there left my. _____

_____

2. grapes ate Anna four. _____

3. wildflowers the Isabelle smelled._____

_____

4. turtles snapping I like. _____

5. donkeys do hay eat? _____

6. water careful in be the. _____

_____

Instead of a car wash, have a bike wash. Gather buckets, a hose, rags and sponges, and car-washing soap that will not harm the environment. Invite friends to bring their bikes. Scrub off dirt and spray out tires. When he bikes are dry, go for a group bike ride.

▶ **Imagine that you are collecting items for a time capsule that will be opened in 20 years. What things would you put in the capsule to tell about your life right now?**

_____

_____

_____

_____

_____

_____

_____

_____

Are you curious about how your voice sounds? Make an echo. Stand across the street from a house. Cup your hands around your mouth and shout a few words at the house. Listen—can you hear someone shouting back?

▶ **Number the words in each group alphabetically from 1 to 5. You will need to look all the way to the fourth or fifth letter in each group before you start numbering.**

1. _____ peanut

_____ peacock

_____ pear

_____ peak

_____ peat

2. _____ greet

_____ greenhouse

_____ grew

_____ grenade

_____ gremlin

3. _____ alligator

_____ alley

_____ allow

_____ allude

_____ allspice

4. _____ iceberg

_____ icehouse

_____ icebox

_____ Iceland

_____ icebreaker

Ask an adult if you can gather some friends at night. Sit in a circle. Hold a flashlight under your chin and think of a story to tell. Mysterious!

► Add or subtract to solve each problem.

1. 24
    + 12

2. 34
    + 23

3. 46
    + 11

4. 67
    + 21

5. 53
    + 16

6. 75
    − 11

7. 87
    − 24

8. 67
    − 33

9. 57
    − 32

10. 34
    − 12

11. 43
    + 28

12. 56
    + 27

13. 62
    + 19

14. 37
    + 27

15. 49
    + 24

16. 64
    + 29

Make a list of things you might see while driving down the highway. Think soda trucks, a luggage rack, a concrete mixer, a flat tire, and an out-of-state license plate. Write a list. Take it on your next car trip. As you see each item, mark it off the list.

► An interrogative sentence asks a question. Write **I** for each interrogative sentence. Write **D** for each declarative sentence.

1. _____ What time will we eat?

2. _____ I have a sandwich.

3. _____ Grant ate a pickle.

4. _____ Do you smell the pie?

5. _____ Who ate an orange?

6. _____ What kind of drink is this?

7. _____ I ate with my friends.

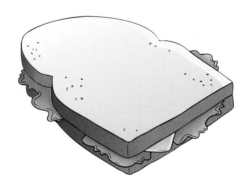

8. _____ Ian cleaned his room.

If you have a clubhouse or fort, come up with a cool club name. Name it after something you like to do with your friends. Or, combine a part of everyone's name and make up a nonsense word. Then, find an old piece of wood or a piece of cardboard. Paint the club name on the sign and attach it near the entrance.

▶ **Read the TV schedule. Then, answer the questions.**

		\multicolumn{8}{c}{Time}							
		7:00	7:30	8:00	8:30	9:00	9:30	10:00	10:30
Channel	2	Quiz Game Show	\multicolumn{2}{l}{Jump Start}	\multicolumn{3}{l}{Summer the Dog}	\multicolumn{2}{l}{News}
	4	Lucky Guess	You Should Know	\multicolumn{4}{l}{Wednesday Night at the Movies *Friends Forever*}	\multicolumn{2}{l}{News}
	5	Best Friends	Mary's Secret	Where They Are	Time to Hope	\multicolumn{2}{l}{Tom's Talk Show}	\multicolumn{2}{l}{News}
	7	123 Oak Street	Lost Alone	One More Time	\multicolumn{3}{l}{Sports}	\multicolumn{2}{l}{News}
	24	Silly Rabbit	Clyde the Clown	Ball o' Fun	Slime and Rhyme	\multicolumn{2}{l}{Cartoon Alley}	Fun Times	Make Me Laugh

I. On which channels is the news on at 10:00?

A. 2, 5, and 24   B. 2, 4, and 7   C. 2, 4, 5, and 7

2. What time does the show *Silly Rabbit* begin?

A. 7:00   B. 7:30   C. 8:30

Learn to twirl a baton. Find a straight stick that is a little shorter than your arm. Wrap the ends in masking tape. Loosely hold it in the soft part of your hand between your thumb and index finger. Hold your arm out in front of you and sweep your hand in a figure eight to make a basic twirl.

▶ **Write the letter of the button that answers each riddle.**

A

B

C

D

1. I do not have corners. I have 4 lines of symmetry. Which button am I?

2. I am not round. I have more than 4 corners. I have 1 line of symmetry. Which button am I?

3. I have 4 corners. I have 2 lines of symmetry. My sides are not all equal in length. Which button am I?

4. On a separate sheet of paper, write a riddle for the remaining button. Ask a family member to guess which button you described.

Secret code names are tsuj a sdrawkcab drow yawa! Make up cool code names for your friends by spelling and saying their names backwards.

► **Change each declarative sentence into an interrogative sentence.**

EXAMPLE:

The busy mail carrier is leaving. _Is the busy mail carrier leaving?_

1. That man is Gary's father. _____

_____

2. She can ride her new bike. _____

_____

3. I will ride the black horse. _____

_____

Grow a new friend! Add some potting soil and a handful of grass seed to a knee-high women's stocking. Knot the bottom, turn it over, and draw a face on it. Dip the stocking in water and balance it in the top of a bowl. Place it in the sun, and wait for your friend to grow some hair.

► **Draw the other half of the picture so that both halves are the same.**

Play a tough game of Follow the Leader for Big Kids. Head to a playground or obstacle course. Let the leader lead the group though the monkey bars, down the slide, through the tire run, and under tunnels.

211

► In a dictionary, guide words are at the top of each page. The guide word on the left tells the first word on the page. The guide word on the right tells the last word on the page. Circle the word that would be on the page with each set of guide words.

1. patter — penguin

panda   pit   paw

2. match — monkey

math   magic   motor

3. bear — buffalo

bunny   bat   bison

4. hammer — happy

hall   hand   hair

5. rabbit — rack

race   racket   radio

Make a beaded doorway. Look around your house for beads, buttons, and sequins. Measure several strands of string that are a foot longer than the doorway. Knot the bottoms and string objects on them. Tie small knots under each object if you are not filling up the strings. Tie the tops to a stick and put the stick over the doorway. Groovy!

▶ Run for Fun and Endurance

Running is a great way to improve your endurance. Put on some comfortable running shoes and stretch for a few minutes. Whether you run in place, in the yard, or at the park, time how long you run. Repeat these runs a few times each week. After each run, record how long you ran. Try to increase the time slightly every week. By the end of the summer, you will be able to run longer and will have increased your endurance.

Take 10 index cards and write a number between 1 and 10 on each card. Give each player an index card to hold up to his forehead, number side facing out. No peeking! Look at the other players' cards. If you think your number is the highest, keep your card on your forehead. If not, drop it. The player with the highest number still on his forehead wins!

▶ Draw the other half of the picture so that both halves are the same.

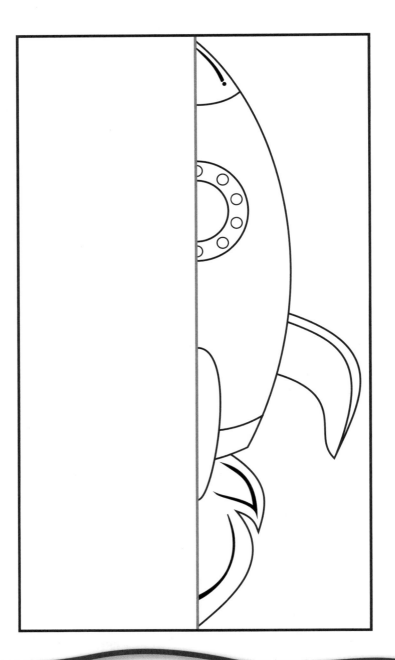

Get your pulse rate up—then measure it. Sit quietly and place your finger gently on the side of your neck or on your wrist. Try to find your heartbeat. Count the beats for 15 seconds. Multiply this by four to get your resting heart rate. How does it change after you exercise?

▶ An **exclamatory sentence** shows strong emotions or feelings. Write **E** for each exclamatory sentence. Write **D** for each declarative sentence. Write **I** for each interrogative sentence.

1. _____ What did they say?

2. _____ I am so happy for you!

3. _____ It's a boy!

4. _____ That is wonderful news!

5. _____ The card is green.

6. _____ Can I borrow a pencil?

▶ Write each exclamatory sentence with a capital letter and an exclamation point (**!**).

7. watch out _____

8. i had a great day _____

Go on a swimming quest. Have an adult toss diving hoops or sticks into the pool. When the adult says, "Go," head out to find all of the diving hoops. How fast can you bring them back? For non-swimmers, retrieve hoops from the shallow end using only your feet.

► **Read the story. Then, complete the picture to match the story.**

Five Flowers

Margaret planted five flowers in pots. They grew fast. She put the flowers in a row. The white flower was in the middle. The purple flower was second. The orange flower was not first. The yellow flower was last. Where was the pink flower? Where does the orange flower go?

Feeling lucky? Look for a four-leaf clover. Find a patch of clover. Think of the three-leaf clovers as triangle shapes. Then, look for a square shape in all of the triangles. You can find five- and even six-leaf clovers too.

▶ **Make as many new words as you can using the letters in each word below.**

1. chart   **2.** start   **3.** craft

_____

_____

_____

_____

_____

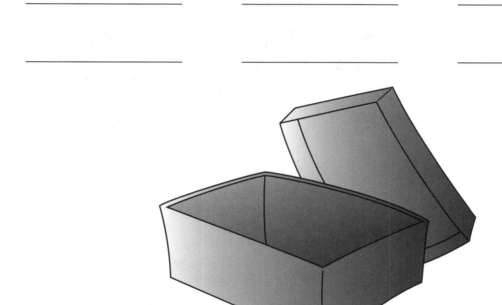

The next time a package comes in the mail, look at the packing peanuts. If they are the squishy, starchy kind, you can make a sculpture with them. Dampen a sponge. Dab a peanut on it and stick it to another peanut. Can you attach all of them together?

217

► **Multiply to find each product. Then, draw a line to match each set to the correct multiplication problem.**

EXAMPLE:

4 × 3 = ___12___

1. 3 × 3 = _____

2. 5 × 2 = _____

3. 3 × 2 = _____

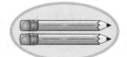  

4. 2 × 4 = _____

Binoculars are not just for daytime. Take a pair outside at night. Look at the sky, but also look in trees and around on the ground. You just might see some eyes shining back at you!

▶ An **imperative sentence** gives a command. Write **IM** for each imperative sentence. Write **D** for each declarative sentence. Write **I** for each interrogative sentence. Write **E** for each exclamatory sentence.

1. _____ Make a card for Mom.

2. _____ Use markers.

3. _____ She will love it!

4. _____ Show your mom.

5. _____ Tell her how you made it.

6. _____ Cards are great gifts.

7. _____ Has your dad seen it?

8. _____ The card looks great!

Make a super snack. Soften a carton of your favorite frozen yogurt by leaving it out for 10 minutes. Spoon a little on a graham cracker. Top with another graham cracker. Roll the edge in sprinkles or nuts. Wrap it in plastic. Put it in the freezer to harden the ice cream, then enjoy!

219

▶ **Read the story. Then, answer the question.**

The Giant Cookie

My mother baked a giant cookie for me. I sat on my porch to eat it. But, before I could take a bite, my friend Ivy came by.

"Will you share your cookie with me?" Ivy asked. I broke my cookie into two pieces: one for me and one for Ivy. But, before we could each take a bite, Jermaine and Drew came by.

"Will you share your cookie with us?" they asked. Ivy and I each broke our cookie into two more pieces. Now, we had four pieces: one for me, one for Ivy, one for Jermaine, and one for Drew. But, before we could each take a bite, four more friends came by.

"Will you share your cookie with us?" they asked. Ivy, Jermaine, Drew, and I all broke our pieces in half. Now we had enough to share among eight friends. I looked at my giant cookie. It was not a giant cookie anymore.

"Hey, does anyone know what is gigantic when there's one but small when there are eight?" I asked.
"No, what?" my friends asked.
"My cookie!" I laughed.

1. What happened to the cookie?

    A. It was shared between friends.

    B. It was lost.

    C. It ran away.

    D. It was dropped on the floor.

Make a fast car even faster. Cut out a square of cardboard and use a pencil to punch a hole in it. Tape it firmly to the top of a toy car with the hole in the back. Stick a balloon through the hole with the "blowing" end sticking out of the hole. Blow up the balloon, release your car, and watch it go!

▶ **A** descriptive sentence **tells details about something. Write a descriptive sentence about each topic below.**

Example:

the young woman ___The loud, black dog barked at the young___

___woman.___

1. a white cloud _____

_____

2. a sad giraffe _____

_____

3. a yellow taxi _____

_____

4. the small mouse _____

_____

Instead of a gingerbread house, build a nature house. Cut a door hole in a small milk carton. Gather twigs, leaves, moss, pebbles, or other natural items, and glue them to the house. Place it outside with the door open to see what moves in.

▶ **Multiply to find each product.**

1. $5 \times 1 =$ _____

2. $5 \times 5 =$ _____

3. $3 \times 4 =$ _____

4. $1 \times 0 =$ _____

5. $2 \times 2 =$ _____

6. $4 \times 5 =$ _____

7. $3 \times 5 =$ _____

8. $1 \times 1 =$ _____

9. $\begin{array}{r} 5 \\ \times\ 2 \\ \hline \end{array}$

10. $\begin{array}{r} 7 \\ \times\ 1 \\ \hline \end{array}$

11. $\begin{array}{r} 4 \\ \times\ 2 \\ \hline \end{array}$

12. $\begin{array}{r} 3 \\ \times\ 2 \\ \hline \end{array}$

13. $\begin{array}{r} 3 \\ \times\ 3 \\ \hline \end{array}$

14. $\begin{array}{r} 4 \\ \times\ 0 \\ \hline \end{array}$

Interview your pet. Ask what he likes to eat and how often. Ask your pet what kind of exercise he needs, and what kind of affection he likes. Write "answers" from your pet. Add a vet's phone number and a contact number for your family, and you have a great care guide for anyone who looks after your pet.

► **Write two exclamatory sentences and two declarative sentences. Use a word from the word bank in each sentence.**

attention	rain	shiver	station
calmly	famous	free	million

1. _____

_____

2. _____

_____

3. _____

_____

4. _____

_____

Learn to do the wheelbarrow. Get on your hands and knees, and have a friend pick up your feet as you straighten your legs. Walk around on your hands like a wheelbarrow. Have a wheelbarrow race with friends.

▶ **Look at each paragraph below and circle the main idea.**
Underline the detail sentence that does not support the main idea.

A paragraph is a group of detail sentences that support a **main idea**. The main idea is usually in the topic sentence at the beginning of the paragraph.

1.
Yesterday my class visited the zoo. We were amazed at all the animals that lived there. There were animals from all over the world in their natural habitats. I live in a house. My favorite animal was the elephant who lived on the African plains.

2.
We played a game in our classroom yesterday called Silent Ball. To play this game, everyone must stand in a circle and be absolutely silent. A sponge ball is then passed from person to person. The ball may be passed to a person next to you or to a person across the room. Mary does not like the game, so she chose not to play. If a player misses the ball or makes a sound, he must sit down. The last person standing is the winner of this soundless game.

Play some stairway ball. Toss a bouncy ball up a flight of stairs. If you can catch it on the way down, give yourself a point. If you cannot catch it, your score remains the same, and if it bonks you on the head, you lose a point.

► **Use the dictionary entry to answer the questions.**

> **germ** \ 'jerm \ *n* **1.** disease-producing microbe **2.** a bud or seed

1. What part of speech is *germ?* _____

_____

2. Which definition of *germ* deals with growing plants? _____

_____

3. Would *germinate* come before or after *germ* in the dictionary?

_____

4. Use *germ* in a sentence. _____

_____

If your sock drawer smells a little stale, make a sachet. Cut two pieces of fabric. Turn them inside out and use fabric glue to attach three edges. When it dries, turn it right-side out and stuff it with cinnamon sticks and pine needles. Glue the last edge together and put it in a smelly place.

► **Write a title for each list.**

1. _____

    robin

    cardinal

    blue jay

    canary

2. _____

    paper

    glue

    scissors

    crayons

3. _____

    lion

    tiger

    bear

    elephant

4. _____

    milk

    tea

    water

    juice

So, how far away is that lightning? Skip count to find out. When you see a flash, start counting. Say, "One Mississippi, two Mississippi," and so on, until you hear thunder. For every five seconds you count, the strike is a mile away.

▶ **Solve each problem.**

1. Maddie has 3 vases with 4 flowers in each vase. How many total flowers does she have?

   _____ × _____ = _____ flowers

2. Mario has 4 packs of gum. There are 5 pieces in each pack. How many pieces of gum does he have?

   _____ × _____ = _____ pieces

3. Jawan has 3 glasses. He put 2 straws in each glass. How many straws did Jawan put in the glasses?

   _____ × _____ = _____ straws

4. We have 4 tables for the party. Each table needs 4 chairs. How many total chairs do we need?

   _____ × _____ = _____ chairs

How much do you know about where you live? Your state or province might be the home of the first candy factory or the only state or province with a professional trampoline team. With an adult, search the Internet to find interesting information about where you live. Share the fun facts with family and friends.

► **Read each sentence. Then, write a period (.), a question mark (?), or an exclamation point (!) at the end of each sentence.**

1. Soon, we will visit Uncle Ben and Aunt Cathy _____

2. Will Jeremy ride his bike to school this year _____

3. That is great news _____

4. Did you have fun at Lola's party _____

5. My family went on a camping trip _____

6. Have you gone hiking before _____

7. Watch out for that bee _____

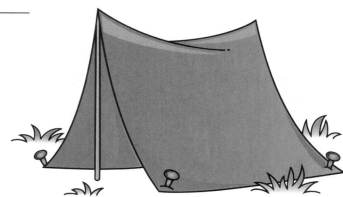

Create a fabulous bedroom—a very tiny one. Turn a shoebox on its side. Cut out squares for windows. Paint the inside the ideal color for a bedroom. Tape up tiny fabric scrap curtains. Add smaller boxes to be furniture. You can design a whole house for almost nothing!

▶ **Solve the problems.**

1.
$$\begin{array}{r} 52 \\ -\ 39 \\ \hline \end{array}$$

2.
$$\begin{array}{r} 47 \\ -\ 19 \\ \hline \end{array}$$

3.
$$\begin{array}{r} 61 \\ -\ 25 \\ \hline \end{array}$$

4.
$$\begin{array}{r} 980 \\ -\ 430 \\ \hline \end{array}$$

5.
$$\begin{array}{r} 543 \\ -\ 298 \\ \hline \end{array}$$

6.
$$\begin{array}{r} 766 \\ -\ 384 \\ \hline \end{array}$$

7.
$$\begin{array}{r} 7,303 \\ -\ 3,855 \\ \hline \end{array}$$

8.
$$\begin{array}{r} 8,624 \\ -\ 4,937 \\ \hline \end{array}$$

9.
$$\begin{array}{r} 5,322 \\ -\ 1,404 \\ \hline \end{array}$$

10.
$$\begin{array}{r} 9,718 \\ -\ 2,579 \\ \hline \end{array}$$

11.
$$\begin{array}{r} 8,972 \\ -\ 4,687 \\ \hline \end{array}$$

12.
$$\begin{array}{r} 5,476 \\ -\ 3,287 \\ \hline \end{array}$$

Challenge a friend to a "rhyme-off." Begin by pointing out an object that you see, such as a rose. Invite your partner to think of a real word that rhymes with *rose*, such as *nose*. Go back and forth until neither of you can think of any other rhyming words. Then, pick a new word and start again.

229

▶ **Read the paragraph. Then, answer the questions.**

Megan's Day

Megan got up late today, so she missed the bus. Her mother had to walk Megan to school. Megan was tired and cranky when she got there. She promised herself that she would never sleep late again.

1. Why did Megan miss the bus? _____

_____

2. Why did she have to walk? _____

_____

3. What advice do you have for Megan? _____

_____

_____

Ask an adult to demonstrate the hand jive. Slap your knees twice, then clap twice. Next, tap one fist on top of the other twice, then repeat with the other hand on top. Flatten your hands, sweep one over the other twice, then switch places and sweep twice again. Finally, point one thumb over your shoulder twice, then repeat with the other. Start over and go faster!

▶ **Imagine that when you go to your mailbox one day, you find a treasure map with a letter addressed to you. Write a story about the letter and map. Who sent the letter? If you look for the treasure, do you find it? If you find it, what is it?**

_____

_____

_____

_____

_____

_____

_____

_____

Are adults in your house bugging you to keep your hands clean? Get their help to make hand sanitizer. Mix one part aloe gel with two parts rubbing alcohol. Add a teaspoon of perfume or cologne. Pour it into an empty soap bottle with a squirt dispenser. Enjoy keeping clean.

▶ **Divide each set of objects into 2 equal groups. Then, divide to find each quotient.**

1. 6 ÷ 2 = _____

2. 4 ÷ 2 = _____

3. 10 ÷ 2 = _____

4. 8 ÷ 2 = _____

Use scraps of paper to make a torn paper collage. Trace a rough drawing on a large sheet of paper. Tear scrap construction paper into small squares. Spread glue over the paper, one section of the drawing at a time, and add the paper squares. Let it dry before you display it.

232

► **Read each sentence. Then, write a period (.), a question mark (?), or an exclamation point (!) at the end of each sentence.**

1. She played ball on our team _____

2. May we go to the park on Sunday _____

3. The movie was great _____

4. We can go swimming on Tuesday _____

5. Please call Robin tonight _____

6. That is incredible news _____

7. Have you met my friend Maria _____

8. Dylan went to a party _____

9. We won the game _____

Quests can be imaginary. Put yourself and your friends in one. Make up a fairy tale starring you. It can have dragons, castles, and knights. Or, maybe you prefer science fiction. Put yourself on another planet. Draw or write the tale, and then read it to your friends.

Read the paragraph. Then, follow the directions.

Lauren's Summer

Lauren is very busy in the summer. She likes to sleep until eight o'clock. After she gets up, she helps her father work in the garden. Lauren reads and plays with her friends every day. She also likes to swim and play soccer with her brothers. Most of all, she likes to ride her bike.

1. Underline the topic sentence.

2. What time does Lauren get up? _____

   _____

3. How does Lauren help her father? _____

   _____

4. Write three other things that Lauren likes to do in the summer. _____

   _____

   _____

Some businesses give out magnets with calendars or ads on them. Use these to make word magnets. Cover the front of a magnet with label paper. Use a permanent marker to write words on the paper. Cut apart the words. Arrange them to make sentences or poems.

▶ **Write a word from the word bank to answer each riddle.**

clock	donkey	table

1. What has four legs but never walks anywhere?

a _____

2. What has two hands but does not clap?

a _____

3. What kind of key has four legs and a tail?

a _____

Roll up a trendy necklace. Cut an old bandana into strips. Wet a strip and roll it into a tight cylinder. Wrap rubber bands around the ends to keep it in place. When the necklace dries, use a safety pin to attach the two ends around your neck.

▶ **Divide each set of objects into 3 equal groups. Then, divide to find each quotient.**

1. 3 ÷ 3 = _____

2. 6 ÷ 3 = _____

3. 9 ÷ 3 = _____

Make art from dried glue. Yes, really. Spread a sheet of waxed paper on a table. Pour out a little glue in several cups. Add a little powdered paint (and glitter, if you like) to each cup, and stir. Use craft sticks to draw a glue picture on the paper. When it is dry, peel it up, stick it to the window, and admire it.

▶ **Capitalize the first, last, and all important words in a story or book title. Write each story title correctly.**

EXAMPLE:

an exciting camping trip _____An Exciting Camping Trip_____

1. my ride on a donkey _____

2. the day I missed school _____

3. fun, fabulous pets _____

4. a fire drill _____

5. my summer job _____

Frame a water picture with water objects. Find a picture of yourself in the water. Cut out a cardboard rectangle. It should be two inches larger than the picture. Glue the picture to the center of the cardboard. Then, glue shells, small rocks, or sand around the edge of the frame.

▶ **An action verb tells what the subject of a sentence does. Underline the action verb in each sentence.**

Examples:

Dino <u>plays</u> football in the fall.

We <u>walk</u> home every day.

1. Small airplanes fly over our house every afternoon at 5:00.

2. The rooster on our farm crows every morning at 6:00.

3. My dad plows the fields near our house in the spring.

4. The ducks in the pond splash water everywhere each afternoon.

5. Mother feeds the chickens twice a day.

6. My brother and I clean the barn every Saturday.

Teach your old dog a new trick. Grab some treats, sit in front of your dog, and hold his leash. Tickle the back of your dog's front leg until he lifts it, then say, "Scruffy (or whatever his name is), shake!" Shake his paw and give him a treat. Repeat five times. Do this routine every day until Scruffy shakes when you tell him to.

▶ A **thesaurus** includes synonyms of words. You can use a thesaurus to make your writing more interesting. Look at this page from a thesaurus. Then, answer the questions.

sad (*adj*): cheerless, dejected, depressed, dismal, down, forlorn, gloomy, glum, miserable, morose, unhappy	**said** (*v*): bellowed, echoed, hammered, harped, mentioned, repeated, sang, shouted, spoke, told, whined, whispered, yelled

1. Are the synonyms for the entry words in alphabetical order? _____

2. What does the (*adj*) after the word *sad* tell you about the word?

_____

3. Rewrite this sentence using a synonym for the word *sad*: *The boy was*

feeling sad because he let go of his balloon. _____

_____

_____

When it is time to recycle phone books, ask an adult to run the blade of a knife down the center of the old phone book, slightly cutting each page. Grab the phone book in your fists. Push your thumbs in the center. Wiggle the pages back and forth to get them to separate. Can you tear it in half?

▶ Circle and write the correct word to complete each sentence.

1. We dressed in special_____for the party.

   cloth   clothes   clothed

2. She turned on the _____ as we came into the room.

   light   lighted   lighting

3. We like to play in the _____ .

   rain   rained   raining

You do not need a paintbrush to paint. Try painting with moss, fallen branches, weeds, gum tree balls, or even magnolia seedpods. Anything that has fallen is fair game. You may need to roll objects in paint and on paper. Compare your nature paintings. Which objects made the best work of art?

▶ **Divide to find each quotient.**

1. $6\overline{)36}$ 2. $7\overline{)42}$ 3. $8\overline{)56}$

4. $5\overline{)45}$ 5. $3\overline{)21}$ 6. $9\overline{)63}$

7. $4\overline{)36}$ 8. $6\overline{)54}$ 9. $5\overline{)35}$

10. $3\overline{)27}$ 11. $2\overline{)18}$ 12. $7\overline{)49}$

Make muddy monster footprints. After it rains, cut out giant footprints from cardboard. Rub cooking oil on them to help them repel water. Attach them to the bottoms of your feet with rubber bands. Stomp through mud, then walk down a sidewalk. Arg! Monster!

▶ **Read the story. Then, circle each word that should have a capital letter.**

Our Camping Trip

mom, dad, and I went camping last week. We went with Uncle seth and

Aunt kay. We had fun. Dad and uncle seth climbed on rocks. Aunt kay

and I saw a chipmunk. We all hiked on exciting trails. There was only one

problem. mom, dad, and i did not bring sweaters. Dad said that it would

be warm in the desert. He was wrong. At night, it was

very cold. uncle Seth and aunt kay had sweaters.

Mom, dad, and I stayed close to the fire. Next time,

we will bring warmer clothes.

Some people like clothes dried outside instead of in a dryer because of how they smell. Ask an adult for a couple of wet shirts to hang outside. Clip them to tree branches with clothespins. When they are dry, compare how they smell to the laundry from the dryer. Which ones smell better?

▶ **Draw lines to divide each shape into fractions. Color each fraction.**

1. $\frac{1}{2}$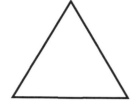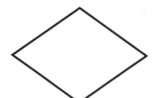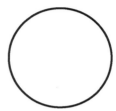

2. $\frac{1}{4}$

3. $\frac{1}{3}$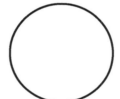

Try thumb wrestling with a buddy. Reach out a hand like you are going to shake hands, but grip just her fingers instead. Both of you should stick your thumbs in the air. The first player to pin down her friend's thumb and count to three is the winner!

► **Read each sentence. Then, circle whether each sentence is reality or fantasy.**

1. A beaver is a mammal that builds dams.

   reality   fantasy

2. The fairy lived inside a mushroom.

   reality   fantasy

3. People can build brick walls.

   reality   fantasy

4. The dog sang a song.

   reality   fantasy

Play outdoor opposites. Go to a park and look around. Try to find opposite events that are happening. For example, you might see a sad toddler who fell when playing but a happy dog rolling in the grass. See how many opposites you can find.

▶ Use the words from the word bank to label the parts of the plant.

bud	flower	leaf	seed	stem	root

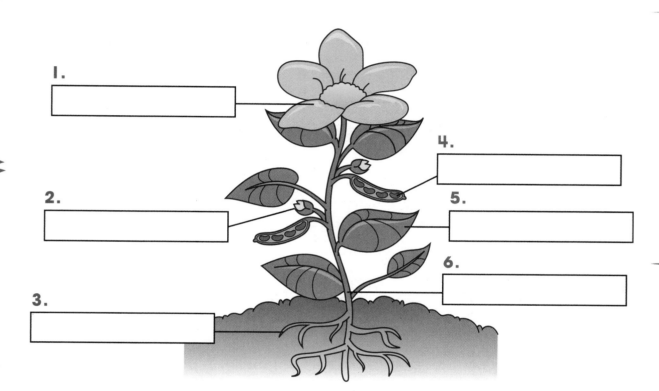

1. _____

2. _____

3. _____

4. _____

5. _____

6. _____

Get ahead on your headstand. Find a soft floor in front of a wall. Bend over and put your head on the floor. Put your hands down to make a triangle shape. Slowly lift your knees to your elbows. Then, try lifting your feet, putting them against the wall for balance if you need to.

245

► **Continue each number pattern on the lines. Then, write each rule.**

1. 1, 2, 3, 4, _____ , _____ , _____ , _____ , _____ , _____

Rule: _____

2. 20, 18, 16, 14, _____ , _____ , _____ , _____ , _____ , _____

Rule: _____

3. 10, 20, 30, 40, _____ , _____ , _____ , _____ , _____ , _____

Rule: _____

4. 5, 10, 15, 20, _____ , _____ , _____ , _____ , _____ , _____

Rule: _____

5. 30, 27, 24, 21, _____ , _____ , _____ , _____ , _____ , _____

Rule: _____

It is easy to add a little flair to your toenails. Paint your nails a bright color and let them dry. Dip a toothpick into a light color. Dot the second color in a design, like a flower or smiley face. Be careful not to smear the design. Give it plenty of time to dry.

► **Each sentence below is missing a punctuation mark. Put the correct punctuation mark in each place that needs one.**

1. Mario had a hamburger, some potatoes, and a milk shake for dinner. He can t eat another bite!

2. Mr. and Mrs Blair went to the movies last night with their three children.

3. Did you know that Maple Ave. crosses Second St at Main?

4. José and Latasha visited Maine, Vermont New York, and New Hampshire this past summer.

5. Don hit two home runs in the game. His team won

6. Wow What a neat costume! I wish I were a pirate!

7. Benita thinks that she would like to be a doctor but she also thinks that she may become a teacher.

8. Bernie s favorite ice-cream flavors are chocolate, vanilla, butter pecan, and maple nut.

Do the perfect cartwheel. Start by tilting forward with your front leg bent and your back leg straight and at an angle to the ground. Raise your hands in the air and fall forward gently to land on your hands. As you land, let your feet fall open. Look toward where your feet will land, rotate around, and straighten up. Practice until you can win a gold medal.

247

▶ **Read the passage. Then, answer the questions.**

Amelia Earhart

Amelia Earhart was a famous airplane pilot. She was born in 1897. She saw her first airplane at the Iowa State Fair at age 10. Amelia Earhart started taking flying lessons in 1921. Then, she bought her first plane. She named the plane *Canary* because it was bright yellow.

In 1932, Amelia Earhart became the first woman to fly alone across the Atlantic Ocean. The U.S. Congress gave her a medal called the Distinguished Flying Cross after this accomplishment. Amelia Earhart set many new flying records. Also in 1932, she became the first woman to fly alone nonstop from one coast of the United States to another. In 1937, she decided to fly around the world. Her plane was lost over the Pacific Ocean. Amelia Earhart was never heard from again.

1. What is the main idea of this passage?

   A. Amelia Earhart flew around the world.

   B. Amelia Earhart was a famous pilot who set many flying records.

   C. Amelia Earhart had a yellow airplane called *Canary*.

2. Why did Earhart call her first airplane *Canary*? _____

3. What happened to Earhart in 1937? _____

_____

Blow really big bubbles with a clothes hanger. Pour bubble liquid into a shallow pan. Bend a wire hanger into a circle. Make an oval if a circle will not fit in the pan. Dip the hanger into the pan and wave it to make bubbles. What else can you use to make bubbles?

► **Circle each word that should have a capital letter. Write a period (.) or question mark (?) at the end of each sentence.**

1. Reid lives in dallas, texas _____

2. mr. javaris is my neighbor _____

3. is caleb's birthday in april _____

4. my mother and i shop at smith's market _____

5. what is your favorite month of the year _____

6. mrs. murphy works at the hospital _____

7. are you coming with me _____

8. my brother's name is greg _____

Tidy up the refrigerator. Paint some clothespins in crazy colors. Glue magnets to the backs. Stick them to the fridge and use them to hold artwork or notes.

▶ **Write the number that the symbol represents in each equation.**

1. ● + 5 = 11

   ● = _____

   Check: 11 − 5 = _____

2. 5 − ★ = 2

   ★ = _____

   Check: 5 − 2 = _____

3. ■ + 6 = 14

   ■ = _____

   Check: 14 − 6 = _____

4. 7 + ▲ = 14

   ▲ = _____

   Check: 14 − 7 = _____

Be neat—learn to fold a T-shirt! Lay the shirt facedown on a bed or table. Fold one sleeve and about an inch of shirt over to the middle, then fold back again. Repeat with the other side. Fold the whole shirt up twice from the bottom. How would you fold a long-sleeved shirt?

Unscramble and rewrite each sentence correctly. Add capital letters where they are needed. Write a period (.) or question mark (?) at the end of each sentence.

1. birds do live where _____

2. very my hard works sister _____

3. swim can like fish a she _____

4. green grass why is _____

5. water fish in live _____

6. park the go can when we to _____

7. the did go she to store why _____

8. is what name his _____

9. love to i play basketball _____

Collect small outdoor objects like a pinecone, a leaf, a flower, and a nut. Look at each item. If you cut it in half, would the two sides look the same and have the same parts? If they would, then the object is symmetrical. How many symmetrical objects can you find?

Read the story. Then, circle the letter of the best summary.

Water Fun

Larry loved to play in the water. Every time it rained, he would run outside to play in the puddles. His dog splashed in the water with him. Larry splashed water on anyone who came near. Soon, his friends would not play with him because he always got them wet. One day, a big truck went by and splashed water all over Larry. He got so wet that he decided not to splash people anymore.

1. A. Larry liked to play in puddles of water. He got wet. He did not splash anymore.

   B. Larry liked to play in puddles of water. He splashed water on people. One day a truck splashed him. He stopped splashing others.

Grow your own yard cushion. Moss is cushiony, soft, and grows in shady places. If you have a shady bare patch in your yard, try digging up moss and moving it to the shady spot. Make sure you dig up the soil when you plant the moss and water it well.

▶ A Life Lesson

To persevere means to keep trying even when something is hard to do. Think of a time when you showed perseverance, such as when you learned to ride a bike. Try to remember how hard it was to learn but how exciting it was to reach your goal.

Take time to help a younger sibling or neighbor acquire a new skill. Explain the meaning of perseverance if he gets frustrated. Talk about how hard it was for you to learn a skill when you were younger. You can also share the goals you have now. Celebrate his success when he reaches his goal. Feel proud that you helped him persevere!

A French braid is a braid that is woven into the hair. Grab three strands of a friend's hair, leaving most of the hair loose. As you cross over each braid, pick up a little more hair. When you have braided in all of the hair, finish braiding like normal. Can you do your own? Does it look different?

► **Circle the fraction that shows the shaded part of each shape.**

1.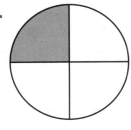

$\frac{1}{2}$ $\frac{1}{4}$ $\frac{1}{6}$

2.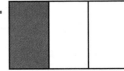

$\frac{1}{2}$ $\frac{1}{4}$ $\frac{1}{3}$

3.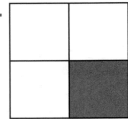

$\frac{1}{4}$ $\frac{1}{3}$ $\frac{1}{8}$

► **Write the fraction that shows the shaded part of each shape.**

4.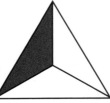

5.

6.

The next time you make cookies, make your own cookie mix too. Measure each dry ingredient twice. Pour the first amount into the mixing bowl. Pour the second amount into a clean jar. When you finish with the dry ingredients, tightly close the jar lid. Next time, you just have to measure the wet ingredients!

▶ **Circle the letter of each correct answer.**

1. Which sentence names three things?

A. Casey took a book, a bag, and an umbrella to school.

B. Casey took a book bag and an umbrella to school.

2. Which sentence names two things?

A. Wyatt put the lunch, box, and book on the table.

B. Wyatt put the lunch box and book on the table.

Take a transportation survey. Go for a walk around your neighborhood. List the different forms of transportation that you see. Use tally marks for multiple viewings of the same kind of transportation. What form of transportation do you see the most often? What form do you see the least often?

▶ **Stories can be divided into two different types. Fiction is drawn from the imagination, and the events and characters are not real. Nonfiction has only facts about people, places, subjects, and events that are real. Read the following paragraph and write *fiction* or *nonfiction* on the line.**

Army Ants

Army ants are some of the most feared types of ants. These ants are very destructive and can eat all living things in their paths. Army ants travel at night in groups of hundreds of thousands through the tropical forests of Africa and South America.

_____

▶ **Now write your own story. On the bottom blank line, write whether your story is *fiction* or *nonfiction*.**

_____

_____

_____

_____

So, it is the end of the summer, a trip, or a family visit. Do not forget your experience! Make a memory poster. On a piece of poster board, write about things you did and stuff you learned. Draw pictures of your experience. Glue on photographs, tickets, or post cards. What was the best part?

► **Look at the index from a book about flowers. Then, write the page number where you would find the information on each flower.**

A	G	R
allium 45	gardens 2	rose 21
aster 62	gladiolus........7	S
B	I	stamen.......6, 7
blossoms...... 13	iris...................8	stigma 6, 7
buttercup 65	L	T
C	larkspur 47	thistle...........27
cowslip 25	lily 42	tulip 26
D	M	W
daffodil........27	marigold......29	wisteria.........20
dahlia 19	P	Z
daisy............ 15	pansy 31	zinnia...........60
	petals............6	

1. tulip _____

2. pansy _____

3. daisy _____

4. rose _____

5. zinnia _____

6. lily _____

7. buttercup _____

8. marigold _____

Uh-oh. You would like to eat a hard-boiled egg. There are a bunch of eggs in the refrigerator, so how do you tell which are cooked and which are raw? Take out an egg and spin it on the bottom of the kitchen sink. If it will not spin, you need to look for another egg to eat!

▶ **Draw lines to continue each pattern.**

1.

2.

3.

Why wait for cold weather to feed the birds? String popcorn and cranberries and drape them over a small tree. Hang a couple of bird feeders in the tree and place a large, shallow pan of water nearby. How many kinds of birds come to the feeder?

▶ **Ask an adult to read one word from each group. Circle each word you hear. Then, read each group of words aloud.**

1. course

corner

cost

cook

2. floor

fix

fire

five

3. instead

inside

into

income

4. east

else

easy

engine

5. begin

behind

began

before

6. point

plane

pickle

push

7. throw

through

those

that

8. alarm

adjust

alone

afraid

9. weather

wagon

weave

weep

Make a white T-shirt special. Ask an adult to help you mix several powdered dyes in large buckets. Loop rubber bands around the shirt. Soak the shirt in the lightest color for at least five minutes. Remove some rubber bands, then move the shirt to darker colors. Rinse the shirt in cool water, then take off the rubber bands. Wash, dry, and wear!

▶ **Draw a line to match the shapes in each group that show the same fraction shaded.**

1.

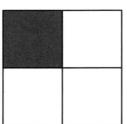

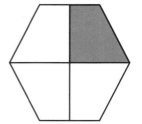

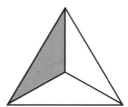

2.

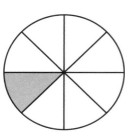

Search high and low for shapes. Find triangles, squares, ovals, circles, and rectangles. Also find cones, spheres, pyramids, and cubes. Have fun looking for hearts, diamonds, and clovers. Try to find three of each. Can you find everything?

► **Circle the letter next to each correct answer.**

1. Which sentence names five things?

   A. Tia got an apple, a cupcake, an orange, a carrot, and milk for lunch.

   B. Tia got an apple cupcake, an orange, a carrot, and milk for lunch.

2. Which sentence names three people?

   A. Alex Lee, Mason, and Spencer were playing ball.

   B. Alex, Lee, Mason, and Spencer were playing ball.

Hold up a mirror in front of another mirror. Move the mirror around until you see, well, more mirrors. How many can you count?

261

► **Read the passage. Then, answer the questions.**

The Right to Vote

Voting in government elections is very important. In the United States and Canada, a person must be a citizen of the country and be at least 18 years old to vote in an election. Not everyone could vote in the past. In the United States, women were not allowed to vote until 1920. A law was passed in 1965 that gave adults of all races the right to vote. When a person votes, he or she helps decide who will serve in the government and what kinds of laws will be passed. Some people say that voting is the most important thing that people can do as citizens.

1. What is the main idea of this passage?

   A. A person must be at least 18 years old to vote in an election.

   B. Not everyone can vote in the United States.

   C. Voting is an important thing for people to be able to do.

2. Who can vote in the United States and Canada? _____

_____

3. When were U.S. women first allowed to vote? _____

4. Why is voting important? _____

_____

Plan a daily schedule. Write each hour in a column, then write something you want to do next to each hour. Mix in some silly things. Here are some examples: *9:00: Eat cake for breakfast. 10:00: Shop for a pet tiger. 11:00: Go to the park.* Which things will you get to do?

Color the objects to show each fraction.

EXAMPLE:

Color one-third.

$\frac{1}{3}$

1. Color two-fourths.

$\frac{2}{4}$

2. Color three-sixths.

$\frac{3}{6}$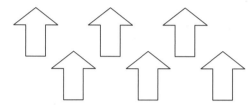

3. Color one-sixth.

$\frac{1}{6}$

4. Color one-fourth.

$\frac{1}{4}$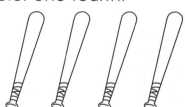

5. Color five-eighths.

$\frac{5}{8}$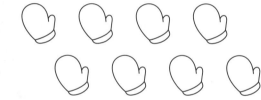

6. Color three-fourths.

$\frac{3}{4}$

7. Color one-half.

$\frac{1}{2}$

On a hot day, place an outside thermometer in a sunny spot. Go and play for 10 minutes. Come back and write down the temperature. Then, put the thermometer in the shade for 10 minutes. Is it worth it to stay under a tree?

▶ **Add commas where they are needed in the paragraph.**

Land Formations and Bodies of Water

The earth has many mountains, rivers, lakes oceans and continents. The Andes the Rockies and the Urals are mountain ranges. The Amazon the Nile and the Hudson are rivers. Lake Erie Lake Ontario and Lake Huron are three of the Great Lakes. The Pacific the Atlantic and the Arctic are oceans. Europe, Asia and Africa are continents. New Zealand Greenland and Iceland are islands.

Do a pair drawing with a friend. Draw the top half of a scene, such as the sky, the top of a building, or a mountaintop. Give the picture to your friend and ask him to draw the bottom. Did your friend finish the scene like you would have?

Write the name of the person who is talking in each sentence.

1. Travis said, "Trent, you need to go to bed." _____

2. "Is this your book, Lamar?" asked Keisha. _____

3. Lamar replied, "No, Keisha, it is not my book." _____

4. "Will you take the dog for a walk, Mia?" asked Mrs. Travers. _____

5. "Would you please go to the store for me?" Sadaf asked. _____

6. "What do you need from the store?" Nina asked. _____

Make a water xylophone and learn how to play it. Line up eight identical water glasses. Add nothing to the first. Add $\frac{1}{4}$ cup of water to the second, $\frac{1}{2}$ cup to the third, $\frac{3}{4}$ cup for the fourth, and so on. Gently tap the glasses with a spoon handle. Can you play a tune?

▶ **Use a dictionary to help you answer the questions below. You will have fun learning some new words and interesting facts. Look up the underlined words and answer the questions on the lines.**

1. Is a goldfinch a bag full of gold or a bird? _____

_____

2. If you were on a jetty, would you be on a jet or a wall along

a waterfront? _____

3. Is a yak a long-haired ox or a person that likes to talk? _____

_____

4. Would you draw a parallelogram or do gymnastics on it? _____

_____

If you cannot get enough of your favorite book, write a sequel. List the characters first. Decide what will happen. Jot down a few notes about the plot. Then, write the book. Add a few illustrations. Share it with your friends.

► **Write the fraction of shaded parts shown in each set.**

Example:

  $\dfrac{1}{2}$

1. _____

2. _____

3. 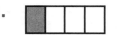 _____

4.  _____

5. _____

This trick is bad manners, so explain to adults that you are on a science quest. Pour one glass each of water, milk, and juice. Place a straw in each glass and blow bubbles. Why do you think you get such different results from the three drinks? (Hint: the drink with protein is the drink that makes the best bubbles.)

▶ **Pretend you are taking a trip to the moon. Use complete sentences to list eight or more things you will do there.**

_____

_____

_____

_____

_____

_____

_____

_____

_____

Fold a foil gum wrapper into a tiny water goblet. Roll the wrapper into a loose tube. Pinch it in the middle and carefully twist it tightly. Fold the bottom out to make a tiny round base. You can make a whole set of goblets from just one pack of gum.

▶ **Circle the correct fraction to answer each question.**

1. What part of the drawing is shaded?

$\frac{2}{5}$ $\frac{1}{4}$ $\frac{4}{5}$ $\frac{2}{3}$

2. What part of the drawing is shaded?

$\frac{1}{3}$ $\frac{1}{4}$ $\frac{3}{4}$ $\frac{2}{4}$

3. Which fraction names the shaded part of the set?

$\frac{3}{4}$ $\frac{1}{2}$ $\frac{2}{3}$ $\frac{5}{6}$

4. Which fraction names the shaded part of the set?

$\frac{1}{2}$ $\frac{3}{4}$ $\frac{2}{3}$ $\frac{1}{3}$

Keeping floors clean is easier now, but a long time ago, people had to make their own brooms. Try your hand at broom-making. Tie a few branches together, leaf-sides down. Tie them near the bottom and at the top. How well does it sweep? How could you make a better one?

► **Rewrite each sentence correctly. Add capital letters, periods, and question marks where they are needed.**

1. bobby has a dog named shadow

_____

2. do bluebirds eat insects

_____

3. may i borrow your video game

_____

4. my name is nikki

_____

As you stand in a doorway, push the backs of your wrists against it as hard as you can. Count to 25. When you step out of the doorway, what happens?

▶ **Use the calendar to answer the questions.**

August						
Sunday	Monday	Tuesday	Wednesday	Thursday	Friday	Saturday
		1	2	3	4	5
6	7	8	9	10	11	12
13	14	15	16	17	18	19
20	21	22	23	24	25	26
27	28	29	30	31		

1. What day of the week is August 18? _____

2. How many Wednesdays are in August? _____

3. What is the date of the last Saturday in August? _____

4. What day of the week will September 1 be? _____

Make a pinwheel. Cut a square piece of cardboard. Cut a line toward the center from each corner to make four triangles. Do not cut into the center. Roll in the corners and stick a pushpin through them to hold them in place. Push the pin into the eraser of a pencil, then tie the pinwheel to the front of your bike.

▶ **An analogy compares two pairs of items based on a similar relationship between the items. Write the correct word from the word bank to complete each analogy.**

| cat | ground | window | ~~water~~ | trees | cow |

EXAMPLE:

Car is to road as boat is to _____ *water* _____ .

1. Bird is to sky as worm is to _____ .

2. City is to buildings as forest is to _____ .

3. Knob is to door as pane is to _____ .

4. Cub is to bear as calf is to _____ .

5. Quack is to duck as meow is to _____ .

Some animals use *camouflage*. They are the same color as the plants around them. They can hide from predators. Dress to blend in with your yard. Go outside. Search for animals that hide in green trees, such as praying mantises and katydids. What animals might hide in flowers?

► Fitness Festival

Invite a few friends or family members to a fitness festival. Set up three exercise stations for endurance activities. These could include jumping rope, running in place, hopping on one foot, or doing jumping jacks. Take turns rotating through each station. Rest after each exercise and sip some water. Complete each station twice. After everyone has completed the fitness activities, celebrate together with a healthy snack.

Be the person everyone hears at the next game. Put your pointer fingers in your mouth. Press down on the middle of your tongue. Turn your fingernails toward each other a little. Tighten your lower lip, take a breath, and blow. You may have to work on it, but this loud whistle is a great way to get someone's attention!

273

▶ **Quotation marks (" ") are placed around words people say in a sentence. In each sentence, underline the exact words spoken by the person. Put quotation marks around the quotation.**

Example:

Mr. Ving said, "Good morning, class."

1. Frank said to Paula, I enjoyed playing with you today.

2. I hope I can go to the party, said Derek.

3. This pizza is delicious! exclaimed Chris.

4. William saw the ice cream and said to his mom, May I have some, please?

Capture a little of the great outdoors. Find a large jar with a lid, and add soil and some small plants and moss to the jar. Next, add a few pill bugs and snails. Put in a piece of fruit and some dead leaves to feed the bugs. Tightly close the lid. Put the jar in a warm place that gets some sun. Watch the terrarium grow for a week, then return everything to the wild.

► **Look at the spinner. Then, answer the questions.**

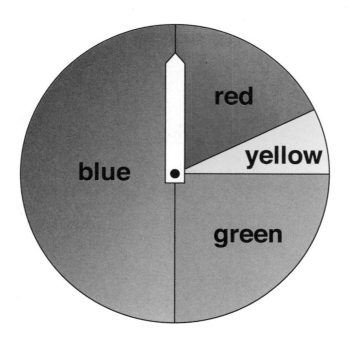

1. Which color will the spinner probably land on most often?

_____

2. Which color will the spinner probably land on least often?

_____

3. Do you think the spinner would land on red or green more often?

_____

4. Do you think the spinner would land on green or yellow more often?

_____

Make your own squirmy caterpillar. Tear off the paper straw cover near the top of the straw. Pinch the straw at the bottom. Slide the open end of the paper down toward your fingers, so that it bunches up. Slide off the paper and place it on a table, then add a few drops of water. What happens?

▶ **Write three sentences. Use a word from the word bank in each sentence. Use capital letters, periods, question marks, and exclamation points where they are needed.**

adult	during	finish	interested
job	prepare	summer	work

1. _____

_____

2. _____

_____

3. _____

_____

Farmers' markets are popular during the summer months because people can buy fresh produce directly from farmers. Create a 30-second commercial for a local farmers' market. Share your commercial with your family, friends, and neighbors.

▶ **Read the paragraph. Then, write the sounds that Nick heard.**

Interesting Sounds

Nick heard the wind howling outside and the phone ringing inside. He heard his mother and father talking softly. His sister was singing to their baby brother. The baby was crying in his crib. The turtle in the tank was splashing in the water. The dog was barking at a cat. Nick could hear a lot of interesting things.

_____

_____

_____

_____

Write secret messages with invisible ink! Squeeze lemon juice into a cup. Dip a paintbrush into the juice and paint your message on white paper. When it dries, tell a friend to let it sit in the hot sun. Your message will slowly appear.

277

▶ The bar graph shows concession stand sales at a baseball game. Use the bar graph to answer the questions.

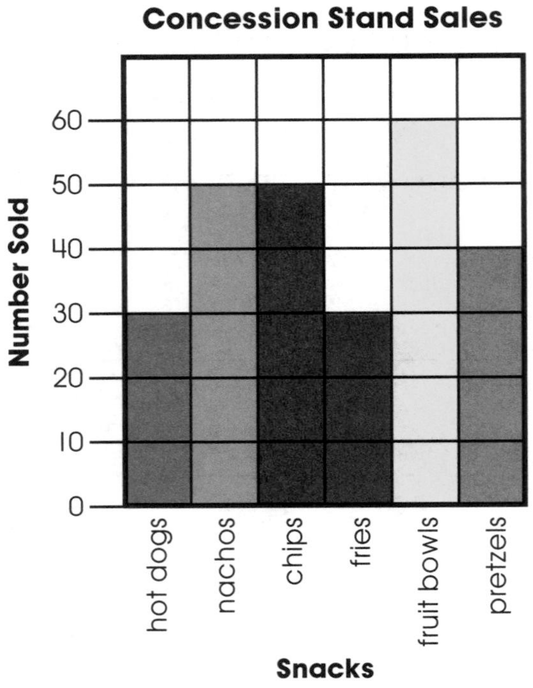

Concession Stand Sales
Number Sold
0
10
20
30
40
50
60
hot dogs
nachos
chips
fries
fruit bowls
pretzels
Snacks

1. Which two items had the fewest sales? ______________________________

____

2. Which item had the most sales? ______________________________

3. How many more nachos were sold than hot dogs? ______________

4. How many more chips were sold than pretzels? ______________

Capture the longest day of summer. Look on a calendar to find the first day of summer in late June. Then, look in the newspaper to find sunrise and sunset times. Observe the sunrise and sunset that day. How long is the day? When will the longest night happen?

► **Use the clues and the words in the word bank to complete the crossword puzzle.**

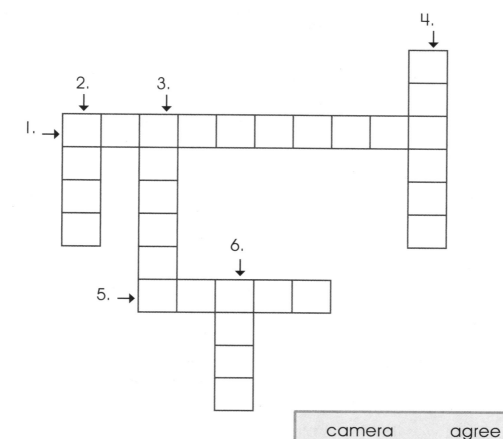

Clues

1. You talk into this.
2. You can drink this.
3. You take pictures with this.
4. People and mice like this.
5. My friend and I _____ on most things.
6. You do this to the leaves in your yard.

camera	agree
rake	milk
cheese	microphone

Going on an outside quest is much safer if you know what plants to avoid. Ask an adult to help you look up pictures of poison oak, ivy, and sumac, and stinging nettle. Can you spot any of these plants? Look, but do not touch!

▶ **Read the passage. Then, answer the questions.**

The Wright Brothers

Orville and Wilbur Wright were famous American brothers. They owned a bicycle shop in Dayton, Ohio. Although they were interested in bicycles, they also loved the idea of flying. In 1896, they began to experiment, or try new ideas, with flight. They started by testing kites and then gliders, which are motorless planes. These tests taught them how an airplane should rise, turn, and come back to earth. The brothers made over 700 glider flights at Kitty Hawk, in North Carolina. This was fun, but not good enough for them. Orville and Wilbur put a small engine on a plane they named Flyer I. On December 17, 1903, they took the first motor-powered flight that lasted about one minute. The brothers continued to experiment until they could stay in the air for over one hour.

I. What was the main idea of the story? Circle the correct answer.

   A. Testing new ideas is important.

   B. Flyer I was the first airplane.

   C. The Wright brothers were early pilots.

2. Where did the brothers test their gliders and plane? _____

3. How long did their first motor-powered flight last? _____

Some say that technology is amazing. What is amazing is how fast it changes. Ask an adult to think back to when he was your age. Can he name 10 technological things that were not invented yet? Which one of them do you now use most?

▶ **The line graph shows precipitation changes during a year in Chicago, Illinois. Use the line graph to answer the questions.**

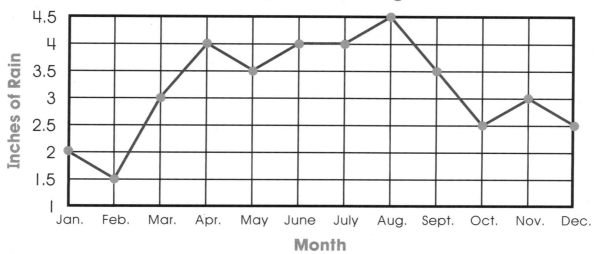

Precipitation Changes

1. Which three months received the same amount of rain?

_____

2. What was the most rainfall received in one month? _____

3. Which month received the least amount of precipitation?

_____

Learn a new way to eat—with chopsticks! Hold the top chopstick between the tips of your thumb and index finger. Let the other one rest on the middle of your thumb. To eat, move the top one only, and pinch food between the ends of the sticks. Is it hard to eat food that is either slippery or small?

▶ **Write the word** *Who, What, When, Why,* **or** *Where* **to complete each sentence.**

1. _____ will it be time to leave?

2. _____ wants to go to the park with me?

3. _____ didn't you do your work?

4. _____ should we go after the movie?

5. _____ time is it?

6. _____ left the door open?

7. _____ does the game start?

You have heard of Hot Potato, but how about Wet Potato? Fill a balloon with cold water. Tie the end. Stand in a circle with friends. Ask an adult to poke a pinhole into the balloon and toss it to you. Pass it around the circle. The last one to hold the balloon before it empties gets a run through the sprinkler.

► **When you come to a word you don't know, use the context clues, or other words around it, to help you figure out the meaning. Use context clues to figure out the meaning of each highlighted word below. Circle the correct meaning.**

1. The green light coming from the haunted house was frightening. It was an **eerie** sight!

   A. green   B. spooky   C. funny

2. We must leave soon. We must **depart** as soon as everyone is ready.

   A. watch   B. go   C. sign

3. The **clasp** of the seat belt was not fastened correctly.

   A. buckle   B. strap   C. seat

As the weather gets warmer, make your brain cooler. Brainstorm a big list of all of the cold words you can think of. They can be nouns such as *ice* or *polar bear*, verbs such as *sledding*, or adjectives such as *freezing*. How many can you think of?

Read the story. Number the events in the order that they happened.

The Alarm Clock

Patrick was sleeping when his alarm clock started ringing. He jumped up, made his bed, and washed his face. Patrick put on his clothes and started going downstairs to eat breakfast. When he passed the window in the hall, he saw that it was still night. "Oh, no," he said, "my alarm clock went off at the wrong time!" Patrick went back to his bedroom and got back into bed.

1. _____ Patrick went back to bed.

2. _____ Patrick's alarm clock rang.

3. _____ Patrick saw that it was still night.

4. _____ Patrick made his bed and washed his face.

5. _____ Patrick started going downstairs to eat breakfast.

If you can find a mud puddle, you can build a house. American Indians and pioneers often had to build houses from mud and logs or sticks. Gather some sticks and stack them in a square house shape. Use mud to glue them together at the corners, and let it dry. Is this somewhere you would like to live?

► **What would you do if you woke up and you had become your mom or dad? What would your day be like?**

_____

_____

_____

_____

_____

_____

_____

_____

_____

_____

Some schools have spirit rocks. Students paint the rock with school colors to celebrate team wins and big events. Search for your own spirit rock. Find a rock that you like and paint it your favorite color. Paint on phrases, such as, "_____ has great spirit!" Put the rock where others can see it.

▶ Study the pictograph. Then, answer the questions.

Number of Flowers Picked

 = 2 flowers

Allie	🌸 🌸 🌸	Beth	🌸 🌸 🌸 🌸 🌸 🌸
Sue	🌸 🌸 🌸 🌸 🌸	Lori	🌸 🌸 🌸 🌸 🌸
Danny	🌸 🌸	Jamal	🌸 🌸 🌸 🌸

1. How many flowers does stand for? _____

2. How many total flowers did Sue and Allie pick? _____

3. Who picked the most flowers? _____

4. Which children picked the same number of flowers? _____

_____

5. Who picked the fewest flowers? _____

Make your own obstacle course from whatever equipment you have in your back yard. For example, you could shoot three baskets first. Next, swing five times. Last, jump off the swing and run through the wading pool. Run through the course five times as fast as you can.

► **Write the part of speech for each of the six underlined words. Write your answers below.**

Vegetables

Do you like <u>vegetables</u>? I like some vegetables. I do not like others. I like snow peas. <u>They</u> taste best fresh from the garden. They are green and sweet. I like fresh, <u>crunchy</u> carrots too. I pick them from the garden. I <u>love</u> corn on the cob. I pull off the husks. Mom <u>boils</u> the corn. I eat the <u>yellow</u> corn from one end to the other.

1. _____

2. _____

3. _____

4. _____

5. _____

6. _____

Instead of paper snowflakes, make paper leaves. Cut out large leaf shapes from green paper. Fold up a leaf and cut a design in it. Unfold it. What has been eating your leaf? Add a tiny chenille craft stick caterpillar if you like. Make a bunch for your friends.

► **The following pictograph shows the favorite pets of students in Mrs. Mill's third grade class. Each picture stands for one student's vote.**

Favorite Pets

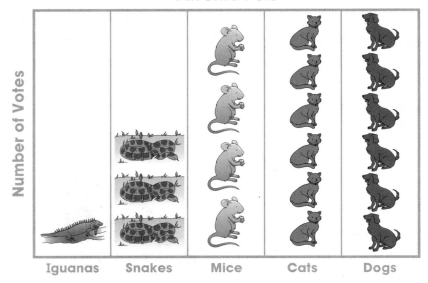

Number of Votes

Iguanas   Snakes   Mice   Cats   Dogs

1. How many children voted for mice? _____

2. What pet received the fewest votes? _____

3. How many more votes did cats receive than snakes? _____

4. How many children voted in all? _____

5. Which two pets were equally popular? _____

Is your grass is getting tall? Ask an adult to mow a maze into the grass before the final mowing is done. Have fun with your friends finding your way through the maze. Be sure you water the lawn after the mowing is done to say, "Thanks!"

▶ **Read the story. Then, answer the question.**

Ready for the Play-Off

Austin was too excited about the baseball play-off game to think about the model volcano he and Pablo were building in science class.

"Do you want to tear the paper into strips or dip them in paste and put them on?" Pablo asked.

"Home run!" said Austin.

Pablo looked puzzled. Austin's face burned with embarrassment. "I'm sorry. I was thinking about the game."

Pablo laughed. "Oh!" he said. "Well, that explains it. Do you think we'll win?"

"My big brother says that Ms. Lee's class hasn't won a play-off game in at least five years. Maybe we'll be the first," Austin said.

Austin saw Ms. Lee walking toward them. He picked up a piece of newspaper and tore it into strips. Pablo understood. He dipped a strip into the paste and smoothed it onto the side of the model volcano.

"You boys should start cleaning up now," Ms. Lee said. "We don't want to be late."

Austin and Pablo carried their model to the science table, put the lid on the paste container, recycled the extra newspaper, and cleaned their work area. They were back in their seats and ready to go in five minutes.

1. Who is the main character in the story?

   A. Austin's brother   B. Austin   C. Ms. Lee

What really happens when you brush your teeth? Drop an unpeeled, hard-boiled egg into some soda or coffee. Put it in the fridge overnight. When you take it out, try gently brushing the egg with a toothbrush and toothpaste.

▶ An Oily Separation
How can a mixture of oil and water be separated?

Materials:

- 16-ounce clear drinking glass
- spoon
- eyedropper

- 6.75 ounces (200 mL) of water
- 6.75 ounces (200 mL) of vegetable oil
- clear glass measuring cup

Procedure:

Pour the water into the drinking glass. Add the vegetable oil to the water. Stir the water and oil with the spoon and observe. Then, let the water and oil sit for 10–15 minutes.

Use the eyedropper to pull the oil from the top of the water and place it into the measuring cup. Record the amount of oil collected. Then, subtract that amount from the amount of oil that was first added to the drinking glass. Record your results. Then, try the experiment two more times. Record your data in the table.

Trial	Initial Volume of Oil	Volume of Oil Collected	Final Volume of Oil
1			
2			
3			

1. What happens when you stir the water and the oil? _____

_____

Ready to go on a safari? Learn about the animals before you leave. Ask an adult for help and use the Internet to research different animals. Research an African elephant. Next, research the black rhinoceros. Check out the spotted hyena! Finish with warthog and zebra. What did you learn?

▶ **Make a graph to tell about Farmer Mac's farm. Color one box for each animal in the picture.**

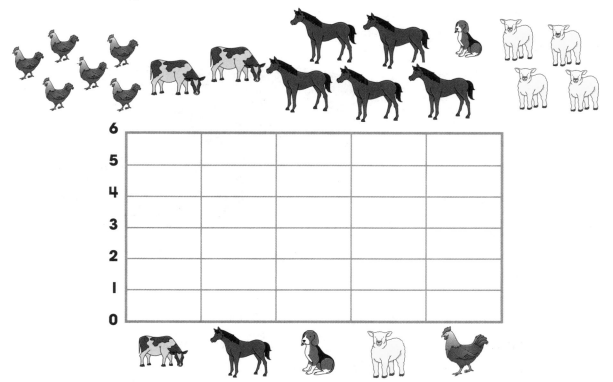

▶ **Complete the statements by circling the correct picture in each box.**

1. Farmer Mac has more 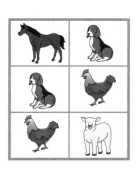 than .

2. Farmer Mac has fewer than .

3. Farmer Mac has fewer than .

Go on a quest to read more books! Each time you start a new book, write the title on a piece of poster board, then put a star next to it when you finish. How many books can you read?

291

► **Disappearing Act**
Water can disappear by evaporating. Sometimes, water leaves things behind when it evaporates.

Materials:
- masking tape
- pencil
- 2 pie tins
- water
- drinking glass
- spoon
- 1 tablespoon of salt
- measuring cup

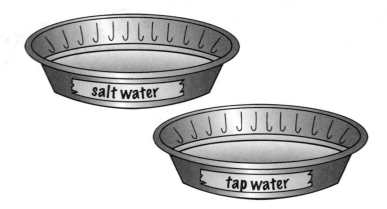

Procedure:

Use the masking tape and a pencil to label the outside of the pie tins. Label the first pie tin *salt water* and the second pie tin *tap water*.

Use the measuring cup to pour 4 ounces (11.8 cL) of warm water into a drinking glass. Add one tablespoon of salt to the water. Use the spoon to stir the water until the salt dissolves. Add salt until no more will dissolve. This is called a saturated solution. Pour the saturated solution into the pie tin labeled *salt water*.

Use the measuring cup to pour 4 ounces (11.8 cL) of tap water into the pie tin labeled *tap water*. Put the pie tins side by side in a safe place. Record your observations each day until the water in both pie tins has evaporated.

What's This All About?

This activity uses salt water as the basis for crystal formation. The water evaporates from the pan. Salt, a mineral, stays in the pan.

If you have two identical flashlights, then you can test batteries. Fill each flashlight with batteries. Put one brand in one flashlight and a different brand in the other. Leave them on and check on them every few hours. Which brand should you take on your nighttime quests?

▶ Land Features
Look at the map. Write the letter of each landform next to its name.

1. _____ lake

2. _____ valley

3. _____ river

4. _____ peninsula

5. _____ volcano

6. _____ island

7. _____ mountain

8. _____ ocean

9. _____ savanna

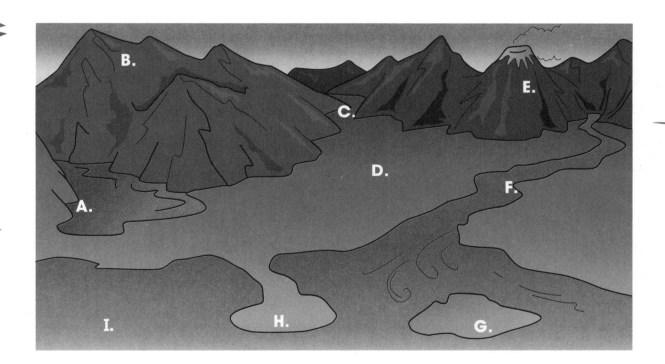

Here are two balloon tricks. Blow up a balloon and then stretch the opening between your fingers. Let air escape until the balloon "squeals." Then, refill it and let go. Watch the balloon fly all around the room.

▶ **Find and circle the 10 mistakes in the story. Write the story again and correct the mistakes.**

Fishing at the Lake

Last sumer i went to vst Tim at the lake. we went fshing.

We went so far out in the lak that the tres and howses lookt very

little. I caught ate fish.

_____

_____

_____

_____

_____

_____

_____

Have your friends do a "feelie" test. Find some objects that feel odd. A shower sponge, a bowl of gelatin, a pile of rubber bands, or a plate of cold noodles would all work. Blindfold your friends and let them feel the items. Can anyone guess all of them?

► **Look at the lines on the grid below. Grid coordinates are formed by the letters on the bottom and the numbers on the left side. If you look at the coordinates (C, 4), you should find the Enchanted Woods.**

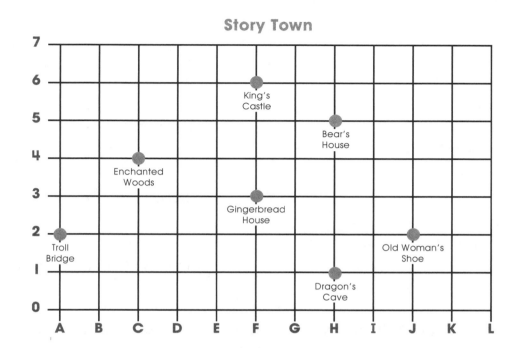

Story Town

► **Look at each fairy-tale place on the map and find its coordinates. Write the coordinates for each place beside its name.**

1. King's Castle _____, _____

2. Gingerbread House _____, _____

3. Troll Bridge _____, _____

4. Dragon's Cave _____, _____

5. Bear's House _____, _____

6. Old Woman's Shoe _____, _____

You can do all kinds of fun things with a can of shaving cream. Drive toy cars through it, or make it snow on your plastic dolls and action figures. You can use shaving cream to clean outside toys, and even write your name. What else can you think of?

► **Countries and Cities**
Political maps show landmasses divided into regions such as countries and cities. Study a map of North America in an atlas or on the Internet. Then, draw a line to connect each city to its country. You will use each country more than once.

City	Country
1. Mexico City	
2. Toronto	
3. Washington, D.C.	Mexico
4. Montreal	
5. Chicago	
6. Acapulco	Canada
7. Boston	
8. Guadalajara	
9. Phoenix	United States of America
10. New York City	

► Choose one country from the list above, or pick a country you are interested in studying. Use an encyclopedia or the Internet to find information about this country. Then, write three facts about the country on the lines.

_____

_____

_____

Let people know you are coming. Use a clothespin to attach a baseball card to the rear fork of your bicycle. Push the card close to the spokes so that it will barely touch them. When you ride, the card will hit the spokes and make a clicking noise. The faster you go, the more you click!

▶ **Answer the questions. Write the answers on the lines.**

newt	star•fish	ta•ran•tu•la
hip•po•pot•a•mus	en•cy•clo•pe•di•a	zuc•chi•ni

1. Which word has five syllables? _____

2. How many syllables does **encyclopedia** have? _____

3. Which word has three syllables? _____

4. How many syllables does **starfish** have? _____

5. Which word has one syllable? _____

6. How many syllables does **tarantula** have? _____

Do you ever give your friends a high five or a knuckle bump? Invent a new high five with your friends. Add several steps to make it cool.

► **Circle the correct answer for each question.**

1. Which figure has four sides?

2. Which figure is a triangle?

3. What shape is the top surface of a can of soup?

triangle   square   circle   rectangle

4. Which figure can Roberto build using exactly seven squares?

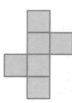

Make a sign for your room. Ask an adult to cut the letters of your name out of cardboard. Paint the letters, then add smaller pictures, stickers, sequins, objects from nature, and glitter. Tape the letters to the door of your room.

▶ **Read the passage. Then, answer the questions.**

A Democratic Government

There are many types of government. One type of government is a democratic government. A democratic government gives its citizens the power to make decisions.

The United States has a democratic government. In the United States, citizens elect a president. The president is the head of the government. The citizens also elect people to Congress. Congress is the branch of government that makes laws. Great Britain also has a democratic government. The prime minister is the head of the government in Great Britain. The prime minister also helps make laws.

1. There are many types of _____.

2. A _____ government gives its citizens the power to make decisions.

3. In the United States, the _____ elect a president.

4. In the United States, the_____ is the head of the government.

5. Congress is the branch of government that makes _____.

If you have a pack of playing cards, build a house! Find a flat, steady surface. Lean two cards against each other until they balance and stand. Make a few more of these. Place cards across the tops of the points. Build a second layer on top of the first layer. See how far you get before it falls like, well, a house of cards.

▶ Take It Outside!

Summer is full of spectacular scenes and inspiration. One of the most amazing sights of summer is the bright and beautiful flowers. Look for an interesting plant that catches your attention or a pretty flower in a garden or field. Instead of picking the plant or flower, keep it alive and pass on its beauty to others. Take a photograph of your plant or draw a picture of it. Turn your flower artwork into a "thinking of you" card and send it to someone you are not able to see this summer.

Math is everywhere—even outside! Watch for word problem opportunities when you are outdoors. For example, if you see 12 seagulls flying in the air, 3 more splashing in a puddle, and 16 sitting on the pier, write these facts on a piece of paper and turn them into a word problem. Solve the problem. Then, challenge your family and friends with your outdoor math problem.

With an adult, find a few different flowers outside. Look at each flower and identify its parts (petal, sepal, carpel, stamen, and stigma). Compare each flower's parts with the others' parts to find the similarities and differences.

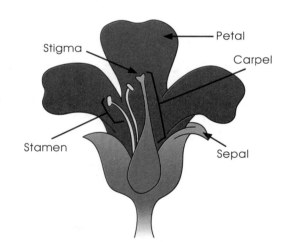

Demonstrate an important science principle. Bend a straw, put the long end in your mouth, and point the bent end up. Balance a round cheese ball snack on the end of the straw. Hold the straw steady and try to blow the snack off the straw. Surprise!

Answer Key

Page 1: 1. 45; 2. 58; 3. 81; 4. 30; 5. 3; 6. 15; 7. zero; 8. sixty; 9. forty; 10. thirty; 11. twenty; 12. eighty; 13. seventy; 14. fifty

Page 2: Students should write the following words under *person*: aunt, friend, officer, prince; Students should write the following words under *place*: city, desert, gym, store; Students should write to following words under *thing*: cloud, letter, plate, shoe

Page 3: 1. 1, 1; 2. 1, 1; 3. 2, 2; 4. 3, 3; 5. 2, 2; 6. 2, 2; 7. 3, 3; 8. 1, 1; 9. 1, 1

Page 4: 1. 44; 2. 62; 3. 21; 4. 50; 5. 3; 6. 15; From left to right and top to bottom: zero, twenty, thirty, forty, sixty, eighty

Page 5: Students should write the following words under the celery: cell, century, city, cent; Students should write the following words under the carrot: cake, cave, coat, cat

Page 6: 1. twenty, twentieth: 2. 60, sixtieth; 3. 36, thirty-sixth; 4. Seventy-seven, seventy-seventh; 5. 5, five

Page 7: 1. boy, shell, beach; 2. aunt, store, country; 3. cloud, rabbit; 4. letter, friend; 5. girl, glass, kitchen; 6. kite, breeze; 7. Anna, book, manatees; 8. Owen, Cass, cave

Page 8: 1. pencil, sundae, helmet, dragon; 2. blossom, rabbit, spider, tiger; 3. carrot, puppy, candy, seven; 4. wonder, summer, cricket, marry; 5. candle, pencil, muffin, circus; 6. peanut, dollar, mitten, window

Page 9: No answer required.

Page 10: 1. 346; 2. 527; 3. 831; 4. 730; 5. 292; 6. 214; 7. 428; 8. 400; 9. 479; 10. 872; 11. 680; 12. 722; 13. 399; 14. 600; 15. 735

Page 11: 1. person; 2. place; 3. person; 4. thing; 5. thing; 6. place; 7. person; 8. thing

Page 12: 1. C; 2. They move pollen from flower to flower; 3. They eat insects that chew on plants.

Page 13: 1. <; 2. <; 3. <; 4. >; 5. >; 6. >; 7.<; 8. >; 9. >: 10. <; 11. <; 12. <

Page 14: 1. mud; 2. camera; 3. bike; 4. bank; 5. hero; 6. palace

Page 15: 1. run; 2. trail; 3. woods; 4. notice; 5. outdoors; 6. happy

Page 16: 1. L; 2. S; 3. L; 4. S; 5. S; 6. L; 7. S; 8. L; 9. L; 10. S; 11. L

Page 17: 1. 2 tens; 2. 1 ten; 3. 3 ones; 4. 3 tens; 5. 0 ones; 6. 4 ones; 7. 7 tens; 8. 9 ones

Page 18: 1. Cindy Lewis; 2. Nicholas Jones; 3. Ms. Cohen; 4. Don Li; 5. Mr. Finley; 6. Ellen Garza; 7. Dr. Monica Seth

Page 19: 1. bad; 2. dirty; 3. noisy; 4. sold; 5. old

Page 20: 1. short; 2. long; 3. short; 4. short; 5. long; 6. short; 7. long; 8. short; 9. short; 10. long; 11. short; 12. long; 13. long; 14. short; 15. long; 16. long

Page 21: 1. 629, 682, 636, 660; 2. 79, 429, 609, 509, 889, 69, 209; 3. 231, 38, 1,639, 530, 333, 32; 4. 54, 151, 555, 250, 58, 50, 255; 5. 1,423, 484, 432, 4,422; 6. 27, 147, 607, 447, 997, 1,007

Page 22: 1. Jefferson Library; 2. Woodland School; 3. France; 4. Roberto's; 5. Fifi; 6. Julia; 7. Renee

Page 23: 1. A; 2. travel easily and quickly from one coast of the United States to the other; 3. a golden nail

Page 24:

1. ⑦816   121   ⑥211
   44   729   ④864

2. 2⑥   84②   46③
   92④   1⑨   84⑥

3. ④31   ⑥43   ⑨70
   1,2⑨4   1①22   2,3⑤1

4. 6 ones; 5. 2 hundreds

Page 25: Students should write the following words under *Noun*: farmer, man, park, teacher, ticket; Students should write the following words under *Proper Noun*: April, Mexico City, Ms. Sho, Sunny Market, Thursday

Answer Key (continued)

Page 26: 1. 7; 2. 5; 3. 9; 4. 10; 5. 4; 6. 6; 7. 10; 8. 3

Page 27: 1. right; 2. one; 3. wood; 4. bee; 5. new

Page 28: Answers will vary.

Page 29: 1. 9; 2. 3; 3. 11; 4. 8; 5. 9; 6. 1; 7. 5; 8. 3; 9. 8; 10. 4; 11. 2; 12. 10; 13. 5; 14. 4; 15. 4

Page 30: 1. long; 2. long; 3. long; 4. short; 5. short; 6. short; 7. short; 8. short; 9. long

Page 31: Students should write the following words under *Singular*: fork, guitar, peanut, pond; Students should write the following words under *Plural*: shirts, crickets, keys, toes

Page 32: 1. re, D; 2. un, B; 3. mis, A; 4. un, F; 5. mis, C; 6. re, G; 7. un, E

Page 33: 1. 2, 2; 2. 4, 2; 3. 1, 1; 4. 3, 3; 5. 2, 1; 6. 1, 1; 7. 2, 2; 8. 2, 2; 9. 3, 3; 10. 2, 2; 11. 2, 1; 12. 2, 2; 13. 2, 1; 14. 3, 2; 15. 5, 3; 16. 2, 2

Page 34: 1. 6 + 5 = 11, 5 + 6 = 11, 11 − 6 = 5, 11 − 5 = 6; 2. 4 + 5 = 9, 5 + 4 = 9, 9 − 5 = 4, 9 − 4 = 5; 3. 7 + 5 = 12, 5 + 7 = 12, 12 − 7 = 5, 12 − 5 = 7

Page 35: 1. tree; 2. apples; 3. treat; 4. flags; 5. swings; 6. sister; 7. pictures

Page 36: 1. -ness; 2. -less; 3. -ness; 4. -ness; 5. -ness

Page 37: Students should write the following words under *fly*: dry, sky, eye; Students should write the following words under *city*: baby, happy, story

Page 38: 1. +; 2. −; 3. −; 4. =; 5. +; 6. −; 7. −; 8. −; 9. =; 10. −; 11. =; 12. +; 13. +; 14. +; 15. −

Page 39: 1. girls; 2. dish; 3. pencil; 4. books; 5. inches; 6. boats; 7. pie; 8. shoes; 9. paper; 10. gift

Page 40: 1. rain/drop; 2. light/house; 3. door/bell; 4. barn/yard; 5. bed/room; 6. snow/flakes

Page 41: 1. 5; 2. 1; 3. 0; 4. 1; 5. 2; 6. 0; 7. 8; 8. 6; 9. 1; 10. 1; 11. 0; 12. 2; 13. 4; 14. 1; 15. 4; 16. 1; 17. 5; 18. 4; 19. 3; 20. 8; 21. 5; 22. 3; 23. 1; 24. 5

Page 42: Answers will vary.

Page 43: 1. pictures; 2. peaches; 3. trees; 4. chairs; 5. dishes; 6. foxes; 7. Answers will vary.

Page 44: 1. 6 baseballs; 2. 2 apples; 3. 5 miles; 4. 12 puppies

Page 45: 1. book, books; 2. peach, peaches; 3. nest, nests

Page 46: 1. A, B; 2. B, A; 3. B, A

Page 47: Students should circle the following words: scoop, tool, hoop, spoon, moon, pool, school, food, cool, zoo, moose, soon, boot, goose, stool; Students should draw Xs on the following words: book, wood, hood, crook, took, cook, foot, wool, stood

Page 48: 1. glasses; 2. paintbrushes; 3. dishes; 4. sandwiches

Page 49: 1. A; 2. I; 3. B; 4. D; 5. E; 6. J; 7. K; 8. F; 9. G; 10. H

Page 50: 1. skating; 2. fading; 3. making; 4. driving; 5. riding; 6. closing

Page 51: 1. men; 2. teeth; 3. leaves; 4. geese; 5. knives; 6. mice; 7. feet

Page 52: 1. 8; 2. 3; 3. 7; 4. 2; 5. 2; 6. 2; 7. 8; 8. 4; 9. 6; 10. 4; 11. 6; 12. 5; 13. 9; 14. 1; 15. 3; 16. 7; 17. 3; 18. 7; 19. 3; 20. 6

Page 53: Students should write the following words under *Animals*: bear, deer, elephant, fox; Students should write the following words under *Tools*: pliers, saw, screwdriver, hammer; Students should write the following words under *Clothing*: shirt, socks, pants, hat

Page 54: 1. street; 2. through; 3. sprang; 4. splash or thrash; 5. split; 6. throw; 7. strong or throng; 8. spree or three; 9. spray or stray; 10. splatter

Page 55: 1. 7; 2. 10; 3. 7; 4. 10; 5. 10; 6. 9; 7. 12; 8. 14; 9. 11; 10. 11; 11. 6; 12. 8; 13. 9; 14. 7; 15. 10; 16. 13

Page 56: 1. It; 2. They; 3. He; 4. She

Page 57: 1. −ed; 2. −ing; 3. −ed; 4. −ing; 5. −ing; 6. −ed

Page 58: 1. 18; 2. 10; 3. 13; 4. 11; 5. 15; 6. 16; 7. 13; 8. 6; 9. 13; 10. 7

Page 59: 1. C; 2. Soap washes off the germs; 3. You can pass a sickness to a friend and spread the germs to your eyes and mouth.

303

Answer Key (continued)

Page 60: 1. 9; 2. 7; 3. 7; 4. 9; 5. 8; 6. 9; 7. 7; 8. 8; 9. 8; 10. 8; 11. 7; 12. 9; 13. 9; 14. 8; 15. 5

Page 61: 1. horses; 2. aunt; 3. bike; 4. umbrella

Page 62: Students should follow directions.

Page 63: 1. I planted seeds; 2. Luke started his car; 3. I put on my socks; 4. We built a snowman; 5. I put toothpaste on my toothbrush; 6. I climbed into bed.

Page 64: From left to right and top to bottom of addition table: 17, 16, 15, 12, 15, 10, 15, 14, 12, and the matching answer is 15 in the bottom left box, middle box, and top right box; From left to right and top to bottom of subtraction table: 4, 6, 1, 5, 5, 5, 9, 2, 3, and the matching answer is 5 in the middle left box, the middle box, and middle right box

Page 65: 1. He; 2. She; 3. It; 4. They; 5. She; 6. They; 7. They; 8. We

Page 66: Answers will vary.

Page 67: 1. =, <, >; 2. <, =, =; 3. =, <, <; 4. =, <, =; 5. >, <, =

Page 68: 1. fruit; 2. José and Henry; 3. My family and I; 4. Marisa; 5. flowers; 6. Daniel

Page 69: 1. C; Drawings will vary.

Page 70: No answer required.

Page 71: 1. 4 flowers; 2. 4 miles; 3. 4 cars; 4. 18 toys

Page 72: 1. listens; 2. works; 3. rides; 4. spills; 5. finds

Page 73: 1-7. Answers will vary.

Page 74: 1. A; 2. oceans, lakes, and streams; 3. when the air cools; 4. soil, ocean, lakes, and streams

Page 75: 1. 42; 2. 24; 3. 89; 4. 14; 5. 78; 6. 12; 7. 13; 8. 0; 9. 35; 10. 48; 11. 86; 12. 97; 13. 6; 14. 14; 15. 11

Page 76: 1. runs; 2. thinks; 3. goes; 4. paints; 5. climb; 6. builds; 7. go; 8. float; 9. watches; 10. eats

Page 77: 1. B; 2. A

Page 78: 1. phone; 2. elephants; 3. alphabet; 4. amphibian

Page 79: 1. 449; 2. 997; 3. 889; 4. 338; 5. 199; 6. 757; 7. 748; 8. 747; 9. 592; 10. 288; 11. 907; 12. 895; 13. 609; 14. 800; 15. 978

Page 80: 1. –ed; 2. –ed: 3. –d; 4. –ed; 5. –ed; 6. –d; 7. –d; 8. –d; 9. –ed; 10. –ed; 11. –d; 12. –ed; 13. –ed

Page 81: 1. J.T., David's; 2. Kendra, Evan

Page 82: 1. squeeze; 2. quilt; 3. quiet; 4. quarter; 5. queen; 6. question

Page 83: 1. 632; 2. 100; 3. 643; 4. 813; 5. 175; 6. 562; 7. 422; 8. 817; 9. 72; 10. 56; 11. 431; 12. 245; 13. 831; 14. 500; 15. 757

Page 84: 1. picked; 2. smiled; 3. searched; 4. rode; 5. asked; 6. mended; 7. mixed

Page 85: 1. jumps in with him; 2. the boy; 3. everywhere the boy goes; 4. Answers will vary but may include: during the day, when a light is on, etc.

Page 86: 1. w; 2. b; 3. k; 4. k; 5. k, gh; 6. b; 7. k, e; 8. b; 9. g; 10. w; 11. gh; 12. w, e; 13. k, w; 14. gh

Page 87: 1. 441; 2. 855; 3. 363; 4. 413; 5. 106; 6. 59; 7. 276; 8. 203; 9. 568; 10. 778; 11. 993; 12. 786; 13. 999; 14. 900; 15. 797

Page 88: Students should write the following words under *Present*: find, laugh, wear, blow, fly, know; Students should write the following words under *Past*: blew, flew, knew, found, laughed, wore

Page 89: 1. F; 2. R; 3. R; 4. F; 5. F; 6. R; 7. F; 8. R; 9. F; 10. F

Page 90: Drawings will vary; Answers will vary.

Page 91: No answer required.

Page 92: 1. A; 2. C; 3. B; 4. E; 5. F; 6. D

Page 93: Yellow Sands

Page 94: 1. past; 2. present; 3. present; 4. past

Page 95:
1.

Answer Key (continued)

Page 96: No answer required.

Page 97: 1. Shady Oaks Street; 2. Windy Way; 3. Walnut Street; 4. Shady Oaks Street and Park Street

Page 98: Answers will vary.

Page 99: 1. 55; 2. 27; 3. 64; 4. 31; 5. 72; 6. 80; 7. 52; 8. 42; 9. 33; 10. 20; 11. 41; 12. 54; 13. 28; 14. 35

Page 100: 1. E; 2. A; 3. F; 4. G; 5. C; 6. B; 7. D

Page 101: 1. 3, 2, 2; 2. 3, 3, 3; 3. 2, 2, 2; 4. 2, 2, 2; 5. 2, 1, 1; 6. 3, 3, 3; 7. 2, 2, 2

Page 102: 1. incorrect; 2. incorrect; 3. correct; 4. incorrect; 5. correct

Page 103: 1. 49; 2. 45; 3. 8; 4. 56; 5. 59; 6. 17; 7. 39; 8. 75; 9. 15; 10. 46; 11. 19

Page 104: 1. made; 2. took; 3. bought; 4. saw; 5. went; 6. flew

Page 105: 1. A; 2. play outside, go swimming

Page 106: 1. 51; 2. 34; 3. 39; 4. 48; 5. 82; 6. 26; 7. 25; 8. 81; 9. 28; 10. 92; 11. 10; 12. 42; 13. 40; 14. 15; 15. 81; 16. 28

Page 107: 1. am; 2. is; 3. are; 4. am; 5. are; 6. is; 7. are

Page 108: 1. leaped; 2. yell; 3. giggling; 4. largest; 5. creek; 6. middle

Page 109: No answer required.

Page 110: 1. 46; 2. 181; 3. 84; 4. 178; 5. 183; 6. 50; 7. 127; 8. 124

Page 111: 1. am; 2. are; 3. am; 4. is; 5. are; 6. am; 7. is; 8. is; 9. are

Page 112: 1. antonyms; 2. synonyms; 3. homophones; 4. synonyms; 5. antonyms; 6. homophones; 7. antonyms

Page 113: 1. √; 2. X; 3. √; 4. X; 5. √; 6. X; 7. X; 8. √; 9. X; 10. √; 11. √; 12. √; 13. X; 14. √; 15. X; 16. X

Page 114: gas, solid, liquid, Matter, solid, liquid, Gas

Page 115: 1. have; 2. has; 3. has; 4. has; 5. have; 6. have; 7. has; 8. has

Page 116: 1. B; 2. F; 3. T

Page 117: 1. 1:25; 2. 11:05; 3. 3:55; 4. 2:35; 5. 10:40; 6. 7:20

Page 118: 1. saying; 2. doing; 3. sleeping; 4. walking; 5. reading; 6. painting; 7. working; 8. eating; 9. spelling; 10. cooking; 11. watching

Page 119: 1. unsure, not sure; 2. unhappy, not happy; 3. unlike, not like; 4. rewrite, write again; 5. retell, tell again; 6. reprint, print again

Page 120: Answers will vary.

Page 121:

Page 122: 1. jumped, jumping; 2. hugged, hugging; 3. cooked, cooking; 4. skated, skating; 5. wrapped, wrapping; 6. sneezed, sneezing; 7. popped, popping; 8. talked, talking

Page 123:

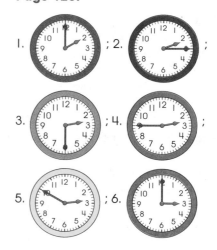

Page 124: 1. C; 2. E; 3. D; 4. B; 5. A

Page 125: 1. D; 2. C

Answer Key (continued)

Page 126:

12:10;

Page 127: I. went; 2. gone;
3. went; 4. gone; 5. went

Page 128: I. more than 900;
2. insects, fruit, nectar; 3. 16
inches (40 cm) long; 4. Bats eat
insects, pollinate plants, and
spread seeds; 4. mosquitoes,
mayflies, and moths

Page 129: I–8. Answers will vary.

Page 130: I. Students should
circle 2 dimes, 2 nickels, and 4
pennies; 2. Students should circle
7 dimes and 2 pennies (all the
coins); 3. Students should circle 5
nickels; 4. Students should circle
4 dimes, I nickel, and 4 pennies
(all the coins).

Page 131: I. stop, stopping,
stopped; 2. clap, clapping,
clapped; 3. hopping, hopped,
hop

Page 132: I. classmates;
2. barefoot; 3. springtime;
4. dinnertime; 5. seashells

Page 133:

Page 134: Answers will vary.

Page 135: I. 88¢; 2. 77¢; 3. 62¢;
4. 51¢; 5. 75¢

Page 136: Yesterday, we **learned**
about colors in art. We **made** a
color wheel. We found out that
there **are** three basic colors. They
are called primary colors. Red,
yellow, and blue are primary
colors. Primary colors mix to make
other colors. Red and yellow
make orange. Yellow and blue
make green. Blue and red make
purple. Orange, green, and
purple **are** secondary colors.

Page 137: I. B; 2. A; 3. B; 4. A;
5. A

Page 138: I. yellow; 2. strong;
3. fluffy; 4–8. Answers will vary.

Page 139: I. beak; 2. eye; 3. feet;
4. tail; 5. wing

Page 140: I. Students should
place an X through the left
group of coins, which contains
four dimes and one nickel;
2. Students should place an X
through the left group of coins,
which contains two dimes,
one nickel, and one penny;
3. Students should place an X
through the right group of coins,
which contains two quarters;
4. Students should place an X
through the left group of coins,
which contains one quarter, two
dimes, and one nickel.

Page 141: I. equal; 2. tiny; 3. low;
4. rainy

Page 142: I. B; 2. a jungle;
3. They were once one large
piece of land.

Page 143: I–5. Answers will vary.

Page 144: I. soft; 2. steep;
3 screechy; 4. hot, wet; 5. open;
6. slippery; 7. soft, green; 8. cold,
warm

Page 145: I. arm; 2. basket;
3. coat; 4. foot; 5. nut; 6. cape;
7. match; 8. shark; 9. whale;
10. yard

Page 146: Students should follow
the directions.

Page 147: I. Students should
circle the guitar; 2. Students
should circle the fifty cent coin
and the ten cent coin; 3. 30¢;
4. 11¢

Page 148: Answers will vary.

Answer Key (continued)

Page 149: 1. Students should place an X over one quarter, one dime, one nickel, and two pennies; 2. Students should place an X over one quarter, one dime, and two pennies; 3. Students should place an X over two quarters, one dime, one nickel, and one penny; 4. Students should place an X over two quarters, two dimes, and three pennies.

Page 150: 1. blue, purple; 2. little, green; 3. colorful, soft; 4. dark, gray; 5. new, brown; 6. white, red; 7. furry, yellow

Page 151: 1. 46; 2. 7; 3. 19; 4. 72; 5. 39; 6. 72; 7. 93; 8. 7; 9. 19; 10. 64; 11. 59; 12. 95; 13. 8; 14. 92; 15. 47; 16. 83

Page 152: 1. 2; 2. 1; 3. 4; 4. 3

Page 153: No answer required.

Page 154: 1. 1 + 3 + 1 = 5 inches; 2. 3 + 2 + 1 = 6 inches; 3. 1 + 4 + 2 = 7 inches

Page 155: A. 1 - Brook chased lightning bugs, 2 - She caught two lightning bugs, 3 - Brooke put the lightning bugs in a jar, 4 - The jar broke and the bugs flew away; B. 1- Sharon came home from school, 2 - Sharon went to the kitchen, 3 - Sharon made a sandwich, 4 - Sharon ate a sandwich.

Page 156: 1. faster, fastest; 2. taller, tallest; 3. colder, coldest; 4. lighter, lightest; 5. warmer, warmest

Page 157: 1. 4 inches; 2. 7 inches; 3. 6 inches; 4. 5 inches

Page 158: 1. A; 2. 8 to 11 hours; 3. You might have trouble paying attention to your teacher; 4. read a book

Page 159: 1. 7 cm; 2. 8 cm; 3. 9 cm; 4. 4 cm; 5. 5 cm; 6. 4 cm

Page 160: 1–7. Answers will vary.

Page 161: 1. C; 2. B

Page 162: 1. oak; 2. six; 3. funny; 4. red; 5. hard; 6. furry

Page 163: 1–11. Answers will vary.

Page 164: 1. A; 2. B; 3. A; 4. B; 5. B

Page 165: 1. we had (or would); 2. you will; 3. she is; 4. we have; 5. I will; 6. you are; 7. do not; 8. is not; 9. cannot; 10. I am; 11. could have; 12. would not; 13. will not

Page 166: 1. 11 cm; 2. 12 cm; 3. 17 cm; 4. 22 cm

Page 167: 1. page 4; 2. Chapter 3; 3. page 26; 4. All About Ants

Page 168: 1. A; 2. B

Page 169: 1. electric; 2. train; 3. keep; 4. truck; 5. play; 6. fell; 7. socks

Page 170: 1. Students should circle the tablespoon; 2. Students should circle the gallon; 3. Students should circle the 1 cup measure.

Page 171: 1. she is (or has); 2. I would (or had); 3. are not; 4. have not; 5. I have; 6. should not; 7. it is; 8. we are; 9. she will; 10. is not; 11. we will; 12. you will;

13. he is; 14. we have; 15. you have; 16. they will

Page 172: 1. C; 2. A; 3. B

Page 173: 1. 10, cold; 2. 90, warm; 3. 20, cold; 4. 70, warm

Page 174: 1. We'll; 2. I'll; 3. We've; 4. We're

Page 175: 1. B; 2. M; 3. B; 4. J; 5. M; 6. J; 7. B; 8. B; 9. J; 10. B

Page 176: 1. E; 2. A; 3. D; 4. F; 5. C; 6. B

Page 177: 1. A; 2. A; 3. D; 4. B

Page 178: 1. Monday, Friday, Sunday; 2. Saturday; 3. Thursday, Saturday; 4. Tuesday, Wednesday

Page 179: Students should follow the directions.

Page 180: 1. December—Dec., Doctor—Dr., Thursday—Thurs., ounce—oz., January—Jan.; 2. Mister—Mr., October—Oct., foot—ft., Avenue—Ave., Road—Rd.; 3. yard—yd., March—Mar., Junior—Jr., inch—in., Wednesday—Wed.; 4. Saturday—Sat., Senior—Sr., Monday—Mon., Fahrenheit—F, Street—St.

Page 181: 1. 634; 2. 8,251; 3. 9,322; 4. 27,800; 5. 70,102; 6. 83,311; 7. 14,760

Page 182: 1. are; 2. bird; 3. bud; 4. card; 5. dark; 6. first; 7. her; 8. more; 9. part; 10. third; 11. turn; 12. word

Page 183: Answers will vary; Drawings will vary.

Answer Key (continued)

Page 184: I. triangle; 2. square; 3. hexagon; 4. circle; 5. rhombus; 6. rectangle; 7. octagon; 8. pentagon; 9. oval

Page 185: I. yes; 2. yes; 3. no; 4. no; 5. no; 6. no; 7. yes

Page 186: I. A; 2.

Alike or Different?	Grass	Tree
living thing	X	X
stands straight in the wind		X
bends in the wind	X	
tall		X
small	X	

Page 187: No answer required.

Page 188: Answers will vary.

Page 189: No answer required.

Page 190: I. H,I; 2. G,5; 3. B,6; 4. E,I; 5. D,4; 6. A,4; 7. E,5

Page 191: I. Dinosaur means "terrible lizard"; 2. Dinosaurs lived on Earth millions of years ago; 3. Not all dinosaurs ate plants, some ate meat; 4. Some dinosaurs were 30 times bigger than an elephant.

Page 192:

Page 193: No answer required.

Page 194: I. C, Africa; 2. A, North America; 3. D, Europe; 4. B, South America; 5. E, Asia; 6. G, Antarctica; 7. F, Australia

Page 195: I. The ice is in the glass; 2. Put the plant on the porch; 3. The lamp is on the desk; 4. Please answer the phone; 5. I will walk the dog; 6. Rain is good for the lawn; 7. Did you see my keys?; 8. Hugo plays the piano.

Page 196: Answers will vary.

Page 197: I. Students should circle the square; 2. Students should circle the square; 3. Students should circle the circle; 4. Students should circle the circle.

Page 198: I. B; 2. C

Page 199: Students should write the following words under *Animals*: fox, horse, monkey, tiger; Students should write the following words under *Toys*: ball, blocks, doll, kite; Students should write the following words under *Food*: beans, bread, cheese, corn

Page 200: I. 6; 2. 2, 3; 3. I, 4; 4. 2, 4

Page 201: I. D; 2. ND; 3. D; 4. D; 5. ND; 6. D; 7. ND; 8. ND; 9. D; 10. D

Page 202: I. 25/B, 37/A, 25/B, 28/Y; 2. 46/D, 17/I, 64/N, 58/O, 49/S, 37/A, 19/U, 47/R, 49/S; BABY DINOSAURS

Page 203: I. I left my notebook there; 2. Anna ate four grapes; 3. Isabelle smelled the wildflowers; 4. I like snapping turtles; 5. Do donkeys eat hay?; 6. Be careful in the water.

Page 204: Answers will vary.

Page 205: I. I—peacock, 2—peak, 3—peanut, 4—pear, 5—peat; 2. I—greenhouse, 2—greet, 3—gremlin, 4—grenade, 5—grew; 3. I—alley, 2—alligator, 3—allow, 4—allspice, 5—allude; 4. I—iceberg, 2—icebox, 3—icebreaker, 4—icehouse, 5—Iceland

Page 206: I. 36; 2. 57; 3. 57; 4. 88; 5. 69; 6. 64; 7. 63; 8. 34; 9. 25; 10. 22; 11. 71; 12. 83; 13. 81; 14. 64; 15. 73; 16. 93

Page 207: I. I; 2. D; 3. D; 4. I; 5. I; 6. I; 7. D; 8. D

Page 208: I. C; 2. A

Page 209: I. A; 2. D; 3. C; 4. Answers will vary.

Page 210: I. Is that man Gary's father?; 2. Can she ride her new bike?; 3. Will I ride the black horse?

Page 211: Students should draw the other half of the picture as if it were a mirror image.

Page 212: I. paw; 2. math; 3. bison; 4. hand; 5. race

Page 213: No answer required.

Page 214: Students should draw the other half of the picture as if it were a mirror image.

Page 215: I. I; 2. E; 3. E; 4. E; 5. D; 6. I; 7. Watch out!; 8. I had a great day!

Page 216: From left to right: pink, purple, white, orange, yellow

Answer Key (continued)

Page 217: 1. Answers will vary but may include: act, arch, art, at, car, cart, cat, chat, hat, rat, tar; 2. Answers will vary but may include: art, as, at, rat, sat star, stat, tar, tart; 3. Answers will vary but may include; act, at, art, car, cart, cat, fact, fat, raft, rat, tar

Page 218:

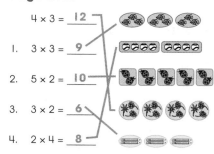

1. 3 × 3 = 9
2. 5 × 2 = 10
3. 3 × 2 = 6
4. 2 × 4 = 8
(4 × 3 = 12)

Page 219: 1. IM; 2. IM; 3. E; 4. IM; 5. IM; 6. D; 7. I; 8. E

Page 220: 1. A

Page 221: 1–4. Answers will vary

Page 222: 1. 5; 2. 25; 3. 12; 4. 0; 5. 4; 6. 20; 7. 15; 8. 1; 9. 10; 10. 7; 11. 8; 12. 6; 13. 9; 14. 0

Page 223: 1–4. Answers will vary.

Page 224: 1. Students should circle *Yesterday my class visited the zoo*, Students should underline *I live in a house*; 2. Students should circle *We played a game in our classroom yesterday called Silent Ball*, Students should underline *Mary does not like the game, so she chose not to play.*

Page 225: 1. noun; 2. 2. a bud or a seed; 3. after; 4. Answers will vary.

Page 226: 1. birds; 2 school supplies; 3. animals; 4. drinks

Page 227: 1. 3 × 4 = 12 flowers; 2. 4 × 5 = 20 pieces; 3. 3 × 2 = 6 straws; 4. 4 × 4 = 16 chairs

Page 228: 1. .; 2. ?; 3. !; 4. ?; 5. .; 6. ?; 7. !

Page 229: 1. 13; 2. 28: 3. 36; 4. 550; 5. 245; 6. 382; 7. 3,448; 8. 3,687; 9. 3,918; 10. 7,139; 11. 4,285; 12. 2,189

Page 230: 1. She got up late today; 2. She missed the bus; 3. Answers will vary.

Page 231: Answers will vary.

Page 232: 1. 3, students should circle the first three and the last three candies in separate circles; 2. 2, students should circle the first two and the last two carrots in separate circles; 3. 5, students should circle the first five and the last five pencils in separate circles; 4. 4, students should circle the first four and the last four balls in separate circles.

Page 233: 1. .; 2. ?; 3. !; 4. .; 5. .; 6. !; 7. ?; 8. .; 9. !

Page 234: 1. Students should underline *Lauren is very busy in the summer.* ; 2. She gets up at eight o'clock; 3. She helps him work in the garden; 4. Answers will vary but may include: swimming, playing soccer, reading, playing with friends, and riding her bike.

Page 235: 1. table; 2. clock; 3. donkey

Page 236: 1. 1, students should circle each banana separately to make three groups; 2. 2, students should circle two oranges in each group to make three separate groups; 3. 3, students should circle three apples in each group to make three separate groups.

Page 237: 1. My Ride on a Donkey; 2. The Day I Missed School; 3. Fun, Fabulous Pets; 4. A Fire Drill; 5. My Summer Job

Page 238: 1. fly; 2. crows; 3. plows; 4. splash; 5. feeds; 6. clean

Page 239: 1. yes; 2. part of speech (adjective); 3. Answers will vary.

Page 240: 1. clothes; 2. light; 3. rain

Page 241: 1. 6; 2. 6; 3. 7; 4. 9; 5. 7; 6. 7; 7. 9; 8. 9; 9. 7; 10. 9; 11. 9; 12. 7

Page 242: Mom, Dad, and I went camping last week. We went with Uncle Seth and Aunt Kay. We had fun. Dad and Uncle Seth climbed on rocks. Aunt Kay and I saw a chipmunk. We hiked on exciting trails. There was only one problem. Mom, Dad, and I did not bring sweaters. Dad said that it would be warm in the desert. He was wrong. At night, it was very cold. Uncle Seth and Aunt Kay had sweaters. Mom, Dad, and I stayed close to the fire. Next time, we will bring warmer clothes

Answer Key (continued)

Page 243:

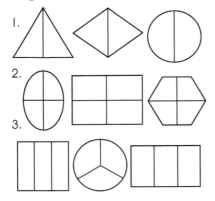

Page 244: 1. reality; 2. fantasy; 3. reality; 4. fantasy

Page 245: 1. flower; 2. bud; 3. root; 4. seed; 5. leaf; 6. stem

Page 246: 1. 5, 6, 7, 8, 9, 10, Rule: +1; 2. 12, 10, 8, 6, 4, 2, Rule: −2; 3. 50, 60, 70, 80, 90, 100, Rule: +10; 4. 25, 30, 35, 40, 45, 50, Rule: +5; 5. 18, 15, 12, 9, 6, 3, Rule: −3

Page 247: 1. Students should insert ' in "can t"; 2. Students should insert . after "Mrs"; 3. Students should insert . after "St"; 4. Students should insert , after "Vermont"; 5. Students should insert . after "won"; 6. Students should insert ! after "Wow"; 7. Students should insert , after "doctor"; 8. Students should insert ' in "Bernie s"

Page 248: 1. B; 2. It was bright yellow; 3. She decided to fly around the world. Her plane was lost over the Pacific Ocean.

Page 249 1. Dallas, Texas, .; 2. Mr., Javaris, .; 3. Is, Caleb's, April, ?; 4. My, I, Smith's, Market, .; 5. What, ? 6. Mrs., Murphy, .; 7. Are, ?; 8. My, Greg, .

Page 250 1. 6; 2. 3; 3. 8; 4. 7

Page 251: 1. Where do birds live?; 2. My sister works very hard; 3. She can swim like a fish; 4. Why is grass green?; 5. Fish live in water; 6. When can we go to the park?; 7. Why did she go to the store?; 8. What is his name?; 9. I love to play basketball.

Page 252: 1. B

Page 253: No answer required.

Page 254: 1. $\frac{1}{4}$; 2. $\frac{1}{3}$; 3. $\frac{1}{4}$; 4. $\frac{1}{3}$; 5. $\frac{1}{2}$; 6. $\frac{1}{5}$

Page 255: 1. A; 2. B

Page 256: Students should write *nonfiction* on the line; Students answers will vary but should be a complete story with correct identification of fiction or nonfiction.

Page 257: 1. 26; 2. 31; 3. 15; 4. 21; 5. 60; 6. 42; 7. 65; 8. 29

Page 258:

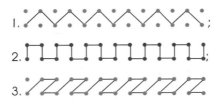

Page 259: 1–9. Answers will vary.

Page 260:

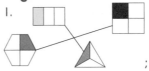

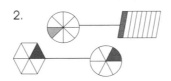

Page 261: 1. A; 2. A

Page 262: 1. C; 2. Citizens who are at least 18 years old can vote; 3. 1920; 4. Answers will vary but should state that voting is important because people decide who will be in the government and what laws will be passed.

Page 263: 1. Students should color in two flowers; 2. Students should color in three arrows; 3. Students should color in one star; 4. Students should color in one bat; 5. Students should color in five mittens; 6. Students should color in three balls; 7. Students should color in one balloon.

Page 264: Students should add commas as follows: The earth has many mountains, rivers, lakes, oceans, and continents. The Andes, the Rockies, and the Urals are mountain ranges. The Amazon, the Nile, and the Hudson are rivers. Lake Erie, Lake Ontario, and Lake Huron are three of the Great Lakes. The Pacific, the Atlantic, and the Arctic are oceans. Europe, Asia, and Africa are continents. New Zealand, Greenland, and Iceland are islands.

Page 265: 1. Travis; 2. Keisha; 3. Lamar; 4. Mrs. Travers; 5. Sadaf; 6. Nina

Page 266: 1. a bird; 2. a wall along a waterfront; 3. a long-haired ox; 4. draw it

Page 267: 1. $\frac{1}{4}$; 2. $\frac{1}{3}$; 3. $\frac{1}{4}$; 4. $\frac{1}{6}$; 5. $\frac{3}{4}$

Page 268: Answers will vary but should be complete sentences.

Answer Key (continued)

Page 269: 1. $\frac{4}{5}$; 2. $\frac{3}{4}$; 3. $\frac{2}{3}$; 4. $\frac{3}{4}$

Page 270: 1. Bobby has a dog named Shadow.; 2. Do bluebirds eat insects?; 3. May I borrow your video game?; 4. My name is Nikki.

Page 271: 1. Friday; 2. five; 3. August 26th; 4. Friday

Page 272: 1. ground; 2. trees; 3. window; 4. cow; 5. cat

Page 273: No answer required.

Page 274: 1. "I enjoyed playing with you today."; 2. "I hope I can go to the party,"; 3. "This pizza is delicious!"; 4. "May I have some, please?"

Page 275: 1. blue; 2. yellow; 3. green; 4. green

Page 276: Answers will vary.

Page 277: Answers will vary but should include: wind howling, phone ringing, soft talking, singing, crying, splashing, and barking.

Page 278: 1. hot dogs and fries; 2. fruit bowls; 3. 20; 4. 10

Page 279:

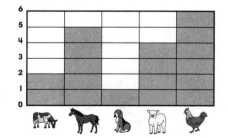

Page 280: 1. C; 2. Kitty Hawk, North Carolina; 3. about one minute

Page 281: 1. April, June, and July; 2. 4.5 inches; 3. February

Page 282: 1. When; 2. Who; 3. Why; 4. Where; 5. What; 6. Who; 7. When

Page 283: 1. B; 2. B; 3. A

Page 284: 1. 5; 2. 1; 3. 4; 4. 2; 5. 3

Page 285: Answers will vary.

Page 286: 1. 2; 2. 16; 3. Beth; 4. Sue and Lori; 5. Danny

Page 287: 1. vegetables—noun; 2. They—pronoun; 3. crunchy—adjective; 4. love—verb; 5. boils—verb; 8. yellow—adjective

Page 288: 1. 4; 2. iguanas; 3. 3; 4. 20; 5. cats and dogs

Page 289: 1. B

Page 290: Data in chart will vary. 1. It looks like they mix together, but they don't—they separate.

Page 291:

1. Students should circle the horse; 2. Students should circle the dog; 3. Students should circle the lamb.

Page 292: No answer required.

Page 293: 1. A; 2. C; 3. F; 4. H; 5. E; 6. G; 7. B; 8. L; 9. D

Page 294: Student answer should read: Last summer, I went to visit Tim at the lake. We went fishing. We went so far out in the lake that the trees and houses looked very little. I caught eight fish.

Page 295: 1. F,6; 2. F,3; 3. A,2; 4. H,1; 5. H,5; 6. J,2

Page 296: 1. Mexico; 2. Canada; 3. United States of America; 4. Canada; 5. United States of America; 6. Mexico; 7. United States of America; 8. Mexico; 9. United States of America; 10. United States of America; Answers for second activity will vary.

Page 297: 1. hippopotamus; 2. 6; 3. zucchini; 4. 2; 5. newt; 6. 4

Page 298: 1. Students should circle the square (first figure); 2. Students should circle the triangle (third figure); 3. Students should circle "circle"; 4. Students should circle the fourth figure.

Page 299: 1. government; 2. democratic; 3. citizens; 4. president; 5. laws

Page 300: No answer required.

Summer Quest!™

Summer Workbook Series

Congratulations!

This certifies that

_____

Name

has completed **Summer Quest**™ **Activities.**

_____

Parent's Signature